# Leading the Common Core State Standards

To everyone's children

# Leading the Common Core State Standards

From Common Sense to Common Practice

## Cheryl A. Dunkle

Foreword by **Douglas B. Reeves**

**CORWIN**
A SAGE Company

CORWIN
A SAGE Company

## FOR INFORMATION

Corwin
A SAGE Company
2455 Teller Road
Thousand Oaks, California 91320
www.corwin.com

SAGE Publications Ltd.
1 Oliver's Yard
55 City Road
London, EC1Y 1SP
United Kingdom

SAGE Publications India Pvt. Ltd.
B 1/I 1 Mohan Cooperative Industrial Area
Mathura Road, New Delhi 110 044
India

SAGE Publications Asia-Pacific Pte. Ltd.
3 Church Street
#10-04 Samsung Hub
Singapore 049483

Acquisitions Editor: Arnis Burvikovs
Associate Editors: Desirée Bartlett and
                   Joanna Coelho
Editorial Assistant: Kimberly Greenberg
Project Editor: Veronica Stapleton
Copy Editor: Terri Lee Paulsen
Typesetter: Hurix Systems Pvt. Ltd.
Proofreader: Scott Oney
Indexer: Sheila Bodell
Cover Designer: Edgar Abarca
Permissions Editor: Karen Ehrmann

Printed in the United States of America

*Library of Congress Cataloging-in-Publication Data*

Dunkle, Cheryl.

Leading the common core state standards : from common sense to common practice / Cheryl Dunkle.

p. cm.

Includes bibliographical references and index.

ISBN 978-1-4522-0392-8 (pbk.)

1. Education–Standards–United States. I. Title.

LB3060.83.D87 2012

379.1′58–dc23

                                   2012002618

This book is printed on acid-free paper.

MIX
Paper from
responsible sources
FSC® C014174

12 13 14 15 16 10 9 8 7 6 5 4 3 2 1

# Contents

# Foreword

In this thoughtful and immensely practical book, Cheryl Dunkle brings the Common Core State Standards to life. For those readers who, like Cheryl, experienced the dawn of the standards movement two decades ago, it will be comforting that our profession has learned a few things since the days of dumping three-ring binders full of standards documents at the schoolhouse door and telling teachers to "read 'em and weep." If the experiment of 50 sets of standards for 50 states taught us anything, it is the essential message that standards documents alone are insufficient to influence educational progress. Although the establishment of the Common Core represents an essential first step toward a clearer definition of what students should know and be able to do, it is insufficient to enact the teaching and leadership changes essential to implement the Common Core. That is what this book is all about, with the author providing three essential challenges to move us from theory to practice.

First, Dunkle challenges us to rethink the premises of teaching, knowing that the delivery of the content of standards is but a small part of the task ahead of us. Certainly content expertise is important, as the expectations the Common Core make on teachers require greater and more specific expertise at earlier grades than at any time in our educational history. Kindergartners will be writing, 5th grade students will be doing pre-algebra, and middle school students will be composing more advanced essays and engaging in deeper critical thinking than ever before. But content expertise is a necessary but insufficient condition for success. Dunkle reminds us that great teachers need effective leadership support. Contrary to the prevailing political winds of educational leaders as those who can quickly rate, rank, sort, and humiliate teachers, the author challenges leaders to inspire, innovate, and implement. Leaders must collaborate with teachers to achieve the depth and rigor of the most effective instructional practices, a discipline that requires focus and energies that elude many preoccupied school administrators and overwhelmed classroom educators.

Second, these pages place the burden of transforming the Common Core into effective curriculum and assessment precisely where it belongs—on the daily work of teachers and school leaders. We cannot afford to wait for any national group, however well-intentioned and sophisticated, to replace the daily work of teaching. Although the Common Core represents a step forward in clarity and focus compared to many previous standards documents, standards without accompanying curriculum and assessments will be a muddle. The essential question is not merely "What do the standards say?" but rather "What evidence must students provide that they are proficient?" The definition and generation of that evidence remains an obligation of the professionals in every school. Dunkle provides a thoughtful framework for these discussions, but her advice does not preclude the necessity for the difficult conversations that lie ahead. Among the many warning signs that the first generation of academic standards were headed for trouble was when teachers sighed, "I give up—just tell me what to do." When teachers disengage—intellectually and emotionally—from the implementation of standards, then schools are left with the illusion of education. Grand vision and mission statements, bold standards, and lofty rhetoric will yield only frustration if the people responsible for getting the job done are disrespected, disengaged, and disenfranchised. They are not merely the recipients of standards, but the architects of their implementation.

Third, Dunkle confronts policy makers and educational leaders who might otherwise succumb to the mirage of standards-based tests as a substitute for meaningful educational accountability. This is the central challenge of our time, as we recover from a decade of equating educational success with standardized test scores. However promising the Common Core may be, they are only a fraction of the equation when schools consider the profoundly important question of what makes for effective teaching, learning, and leadership. The author reminds us that while student proficiency in the Common Core is essential as a matter of securing our nation's future, the accountability for that success is not merely the sum of the test scores of children, but rather the product of a complex set of variables that includes the adults—parents, teachers, and school leaders.

Cheryl Dunkle has devoted a lifetime to supporting the ideals expressed in this book, and readers who take the time to study, discuss, and learn from her years of wisdom will find their investment of time and energy well rewarded.

—*Douglas B. Reeves*
*Boston, Massachusetts*

# Preface

*I can never fear that things will go far wrong*
*where common sense has fair play.*

—Thomas Jefferson

## FROM COMMON SENSE

This book has been rattling around in my head for years. My work as a classroom teacher, practicing principal, professional development consultant, and college instructor has brought me to this point in my thinking about school leadership and the educational transformations that are critical for our students to learn more successfully and our teachers to teach more effectively. The impetus for me to actually pick up a pen and plug in my computer to convey some ideas and thoughts on a page resurfaced when the Common Core State Standards (CCSS) were recently adopted by 46 states and the District of Columbia. Now I feel compelled to write.

After extensive review of the literature about excellence in the schoolhouse, deep discussions with my colleagues at the Leadership and Learning Center, and my successful 40-year career in this profession, I continue to ask myself, if we know so much about what is essential for our students' learning successes and all of the research supports similar conclusions, why isn't this *common sense* translated into *common practice* in America's schools? This question provides me with the renewed motivation to keep on reading, reviewing, and reflecting to offer some suggestions about creating schools that will welcome the Common Core State Standards initiative with an open mind and work diligently to get it right this time.

I agree with Secretary of Education Arne Duncan when he states that the CCSS reform initiative is indeed our "moon shot" in American education. If we do not embrace this opportunity to build upon the courageous and challenging work of the authors of Common Core State Standards, our momentum and enthusiasm to create meaningful change in how we educate our students will wane just as it did in 1992 and 1997. Both the Republican and Democratic parties, with laudable and best intentions, failed to define our common national learning targets as they had pledged they would do. We cannot afford for that legislative stalemate to occur again in our country. As educators, we must contribute our talent, our energy, and our expertise to this vital educational initiative.

Many deeply caring and invested Americans are engaged in the current debate about the benefit and worth of the recently created and widely adopted Common Core State Standards as a viable education reform. Provocative and reflective questions arise in many of these vibrant and animated conversations.

- Will CCSS cure the unevenness of educational opportunity and quality across our nation?
- Will CCSS dramatically improve the mediocre performance of our students on international assessments?
- Will the new standards provide some consistency in comparing student readiness for college, careers, and citizenship from state to state?
- Are the CCSS more rigorous than what already exist in certain states?
- Is the CCSS initiative an organic process for educational improvement and accountability or just another stand-alone educational reform?

Great questions, right? In order for educators to answer in the affirmative to all five critical inquiries, we must first ensure that we thoughtfully consider five additional strategic implementation issues.

- What are the implications for curriculum, instruction, and assessment decision making in the structure of the new standards?
- What realities and challenges do school leaders face in transitioning their schools and districts to CCSS?
- How will school leaders communicate and promote the message of CCSS so that teachers will work diligently to infuse them into their daily instruction and parents will embrace them as a workable alternative to what they are familiar with?
- Which current teaching and learning practices and leadership policies will remain the same and which will need to be modified or abandoned?
- What types of additional resources and supports are necessary for the successful implementation of this initiative?

Opinions and responses to these preliminary concerns and questions are as diverse as the adults sharing them. Many educators, parents, community leaders, and policy makers are saying it is about time we agree as a nation on what our students need to know and be able to do at each level of a K–12 public school experience. Others contend that this initiative smacks of an attempt to federalize what is constitutionally a state's right and responsibility to determine, and national standards will limit the innovation and flexibility in local decision making. One of the dissenters in my own state of Colorado likened the approval of CCSS to being as naive as taking out a home mortgage without knowing the terms of the loan.

Whichever argument you accept as truth about the potential power of this historic reform determines your role as a firm supporter or tentative skeptic of CCSS, and I believe both perspectives are necessary to enhance the outreach and quality of the final solution. Your responsibility as a school or teacher leader in the participating 46 states and Washington, D.C., nonetheless, is to ensure that this standards-based dialogue translates to common core accountability in each of your classrooms, which now comprise 85% of our nation's students.

With its admitted flaws, design challenges, and unresolved issues, CCSS still represents our moral and ethical promise to do better for our children and the pledge that we should work together to keep. Our collective responsibility as educators and policy makers is to ensure that all of our students are prepared and on target for their next level of learning. As of today, many are not. Every citizen must respond to this call for action, and as school leaders and practitioners we must be first in line to propose and promote the right work and the right way to accomplish it.

## TO COMMON PRACTICE

I take very seriously what I am attempting to do with this book. Apt and appropriate words can ignite a fire within each reader to move right past what is and go directly to what can be. That is what I want to inspire. It's a pretty tall order for a rookie writer, but perhaps my passion overshadows my practicality right now. I know from experience we can create standards-based schools that support the success of all students. I agree with Douglas Reeves, my leader and mentor at the Leadership and Learning Center, and many other prominent educators and researchers who believe we already possess the knowledge and ability necessary to answer the difficult questions and solve the challenging problems of CCSS implementation; we just need to make a plan and get busy. In a thoughtful manner, we can move *from common sense to common practice.*

The landscape of education is going to change dramatically during the next decade with or without our collective professional energy and expertise. States that adopt CCSS and even those few who decline the invitation to join this reform initiative will influence our primary work for the next 5 to 10 years and beyond. Preparing our teachers to be ready and willing to embrace these new standards, refining our curriculum and instruction to match the rigor of CCSS, creating next-generation assessment systems to measure our effectiveness at reaching the ambitious goals of CCSS, and designing an educational accountability system to connect all of these separate pieces in a logical way is a leader's challenge for years to come.

The nine chapters in this book do not represent any innovative quick fix or shortcut solutions for improving teaching and learning. My experience as an educator says there aren't any. They do, however, encourage necessary conversations about what our obligations are in supporting new levels of achievement and performance from all of America's students and provide some concrete implementation suggestions to help us get there. I believe the adoption of CCSS is a first step in meeting the commitment of providing excellence and equity of opportunity to every student. Perhaps providing new insight on an old issue or offering old insight on a new issue, depending on your perspective, is the intent of the following chapters. New and different is intimidating to many people, but if we can connect the known to the unknown, if we can determine what already works for our students and what needs repair, these necessary changes will become less threatening and more plausible. And isn't that, in fact, the definition of learning for all of us?

## CHAPTER 1: WHAT MATTERS MOST

I begin this book deliberately not with the typical description of the CCSS initiative but with the respectful and honest acknowledgment that teachers assume the starring role in any school reform. Classroom teachers have the power to propel or postpone any change initiative that ultimately impacts students. That is why we must consciously ensure that our best teachers have a platform from which to speak on behalf of their potential work with Common Core State Standards. We must blur the lines of traditional leadership so that the voices of these adults who matter most can be heard over the white noise that might distract us from effective implementation of CCSS. Chapter 1 helps us imagine a brighter future for our students by identifying the present realities that classroom teachers face on a daily basis.

## CHAPTER 2: LEADING WITH ROOTS AND WINGS

Educational reform initiatives come and go, but the ones with staying power and influence must have the endorsement of the school principal. Any change effort cannot survive a principal's opposition or indifference. Chapter 2 discusses the importance of bold and visionary leadership to initiate and sustain the compelling conversations that encourage and cultivate great teaching in a building. Supporting teachers is neither dramatic nor easy work, but it is imperative if we are to remove the boundaries of scattered pockets of excellence in our schools. Skillful leaders create collaborative structures and a climate of trust to share professional expertise and expand the capacity of every staff member in the building. Both are critical to the successful implementation of CCSS.

## CHAPTER 3: THE PROMISES AND POSSIBILITIES OF COMMON CORE STATE STANDARDS

In response to the confidence crisis in the American public educational system from President Obama on down, the National Governors Association and the Council of Chief State School Officers released Common Core State Standards for grades K–12 in English language arts and mathematics in June 2010. The state-led initiative to develop these standards grew out of concerns that the current policy of 50 different sets of standards in 50 states is not adequately preparing students with the necessary knowledge and skills to compete globally in our highly mobile society. This chapter delves deeper into the CCSS initiative and discusses what is explicitly stated in the document and what strategic planning is left to the discretion of individual districts and schools.

## CHAPTER 4: A RELEVANT AND RIGOROUS COMMON CORE CURRICULUM

Gone are the days when rearranging and revising what has been traditionally taught in schools is appropriate in curriculum design. School systems will have two distinct options to deal with aligning a relevant and rigorous curriculum to CCSS. Perhaps a district has adequate funding to purchase commercially produced curricular programs that demonstrate close "cross walking" to CCSS. Or perhaps a school system elects to customize existing materials and resources to update and redesign curricula to support the new standards. Either choice mandates that knowledgeable content specialists test their assumptions and attitudes about creating the "what" of learning. Since we will not have the benefit of the high-stakes assessments available prior to the implementation of the standards, we will need to conduct deep discussions and debates about what knowledge is enduring, what knowledge is essential, and what knowledge needs new emphasis to ensure that our students are college and career ready. This is the topic of Chapter 4.

## CHAPTER 5: INVITING STUDENTS TO LEARN

Perhaps the most contentious issue about the CCSS document for many educators is the dissension about whether research-based practices in instructional strategies should have been included in the recommendations for implementation. The authors of CCSS have been challenged by their controversial stance that "teachers are thus free to provide students with whatever tools and knowledge their professional judgment and experience identify as most helpful for meeting the goals set out in the Standards" (Common Core State Standards Initiative, n.d.). The standards define what all students are expected to know and be able to do but not how teachers should teach. Discussions in Chapter 5 address both components of effective education—content and process—and add some suggestions for avoiding the potential disruption to the delicate balance between the art and science of teaching.

## CHAPTER 6: POWERFUL PROFESSIONAL LEARNING FOR ADULTS

Since research shows educator quality to be the most important school influence on student achievement, it seems logical that teachers will require ongoing, sustained opportunities to enhance their knowledge and skills to teach all children more effectively in their classrooms. The dilemma is agreeing on how to effectively accomplish this task. Low-quality and unfocused trainings have left some teachers with limited faith that staff development activities can actually help them in their daily interaction with students. Professional development that is most effective in improving educator practice is results oriented, data driven, constructivist in nature, and job embedded. Chapter 6 explores methods and models to structure meaningful and worthwhile professional learning opportunities to support the implementation of CCSS.

## CHAPTER 7: NEXT-GENERATION ASSESSMENT SYSTEMS

There is a shared anonymous adage among educators that states: "What is inspected is expected and what is expected should be inspected." Two consortia of states have a historic opportunity to use Race to the Top funds to create next-generation assessment systems that can better fulfill the many purposes we have for testing: providing rich formative data that can inform decision making while also inspiring high-quality instruction in classrooms, allowing comparisons of student proficiency from state to state, and creating more rigorous and relevant performance tasks to measure authentic and ongoing student learning. Chapter 7 addresses how the next generation of state assessments can make the CCSS concrete and meaningful to educators, students, and parents and provide a critical vehicle for ensuring that all students master essential knowledge and skills and educators can be accountable for the results.

## CHAPTER 8: POWERFUL LEARNING THROUGH POWERFUL TECHNOLOGY

Advanced technology, which is pervasive in every aspect of our personal and professional lives, dictates that we interact and work differently. Leveraging the power of media literacy to instruct and assess learning will be a vital consideration to enhance the learning opportunities for all of our students. There is prolific electronic content and digital interactivity everywhere but in most of our schools. Many students believe that more learning takes places outside of the brick-and-mortar institutions: They suspend their expectations of learning something valuable and meaningful until the final bell rings at the end of their formal school day when they are once again allowed to turn on all of their mobile electronic devices. Harnessing the potential of technology as a tool to change our entire educational system from the classroom to the state offices is a must and the subject of Chapter 8.

## CHAPTER 9: ACCOUNTABILITY FOR EXCELLENCE AND EQUITY

Educational accountability, to me, simply represents any effort to document progress toward the goal of improved student learning and academic success. Sadly, most people's experience with the word is reduced to critically viewing numbers on a page that list test scores on a required high-stakes exam. Just as a portfolio is a better indicator of student progress over time, so is a multidimensional accountability system more valid as a record of results in teaching, learning, and leadership. The report should include not only how well the students are doing, but also how the adults' actions support their growth. Chapter 9 demonstrates how teachers and school leaders can take control of the accountability mandates to ensure that they are meaningful and relevant to the real work of schools. Excellent teachers do not resist responsibility for student success—they welcome and celebrate it—and are constantly investigating more effective ways of engaging everyone in the accountability process.

So that's the book. As you can see, it is not a training manual, not a treatise on the history of educational standards. It is a practitioner's thoughts on the tremendous potential that Common Core State Standards offers our struggling educational system. Hopefully, as a result of reading these pages for authenticity, thinking deeply about the contents, and discussing the book passionately and purposefully with colleagues, CCSS will become a valuable and viable education reform reality. We can finally fulfill a promise to our youth to guarantee that if they work hard and we do our part, America can commemorate the first generation of students in our nation's history that is fully prepared to meet the challenges of the future and best positioned to compete successfully as global citizens.

You might be asking yourself these questions as you evaluate this book's relevance and potential contribution to inform your CCSS work:

- Is this manuscript intended to generate ideas and discussion topics to inform the potential work of implementing CCSS?
- Does this book contain both the bias and the benefit of an experienced and successful educator?
- Is this book written with the passion and pride of someone hopeful for the future of American education?
- Will the book inspire school leaders who are invested in the potential of our students to reach higher levels of achievement and performance?

The answers to your queries are yes; probably; you bet; and hopefully so. With incredibly difficult and deliberate work ahead that requires huge displays of efficacy, I optimistically believe we can achieve those positive differences in teaching, learning, and leadership that drive our passion to change the world for our students. The following chapters and subsequent discussions will hopefully focus our effort and energy on the critical issues and intelligently inform the decisions that result. This book certainly does not represent an all-inclusive list of considerations for implementing CCSS, but it does represent my attempt to launch some of the compelling conversations that need to be hosted by school leaders. You, as the reader, can take what you need, what makes sense to you, and what fits with your values, beliefs, and experiences.

Let's roll up our sleeves, lean in, and push forward together.

# Acknowledgments

The more I look at the world, the more I recognize that when I think about what I now value, it is no longer about acquiring things. It is about appreciating family, friends, love, freedom, health, happiness, time, and security. I attribute this change in my insight to maturity and to many rich professional and personal experiences along the way.

This book represents this enhanced outlook on life, and I want to acknowledge and thank three very important families that contributed to it and collectively helped me achieve my dream of writing and publishing. This sincere thank-you note begins with my friends and colleagues in Douglas County Schools, where I spent the majority of my career in education. This group of dedicated and innovative educators grew me as a leader and taught me how to do the work of learning, teaching, and leading with an open mind and heart. Thank you to everyone who tolerated my impulsivity and called it enthusiasm.

The Leadership and Learning Center receives my second and heartfelt appreciation for growing me as a thinker. The immense pool of talented people that I have learned from the past 10 years has allowed me to see a clearer journey and a more hopeful destination for our students. Thank you for asking for my thoughts and inviting me to join a very powerful think tank of caring and compassionate educators.

Finally, and most importantly, I want to thank my Dunkle family for just growing me as a person, a wife, a mom, a nana, and a mother-in-law. Each of you has pushed me when I was stuck, pulled me when I was reluctant, and stood beside me always. Thank you, Wayne, Jason, Megan, Kyler, Madison, Mackenzie, Morgan, Cindy, and Chris.

## PUBLISHER'S ACKNOWLEDGMENTS

Corwin would like to thank the following individuals for taking the time to provide their editorial insight and guidance:

Charlotte R. Bihm, Grants Facilitator
St. Landry Parish School Board
Opelousas, Louisiana

Freda Hicks, Assistant Principal
Grady Brown Elementary School
Hillsborough, North Carolina

Martin J. Hudacs, Superintendent
Solanco School District
Quarryville, Pennsylvania

Delia McCraley, Principal
Southgate Academy Charter School
Tucson, Arizona

Richard Rutledge, Assistant Principal
Arab High School
Arab, Alabama

Jason Thompson, Assistant Principal
Schalmont Central School District
Schenectady, New York

Bonnie Tryon, Retired Principal
Cobleskill-Richmondville Central School
Cobleskill, New York

# About the Author

 **Cheryl A. Dunkle** is a professional development associate with the Leadership and Learning Center, located in Englewood, Colorado, working with educators across the country in the areas of assessment, accountability, and standards implementation. She was a practicing elementary principal with Douglas County Schools from 1983 to 2001. Previous to that, she served as an elementary guidance counselor and a teacher of primary students for 14 years. She retired from public education in July 2001.

In addition to her leadership in public schools, Cheryl has taught for several colleges and universities both online and in face-to-face courses and has coordinated a cohort teacher education program in the Denver metro area. Cheryl has a wealth of experience with professional development, including work as a district trainer of trainers in the areas of early childhood education, effective teaching strategies, group facilitation, Cognitive Coaching, student discipline, and techniques for success in working with parents. She has extensive knowledge in adult development and learning theory, as well as standards-based education and data-driven decision making. Her current area of study and interest is investigating the elements of successful implementation of the Common Core State Standards.

Recognitions for her work include National Distinguished Principal, president of the Colorado Association of Elementary School Principals and recipient of their department service award, member of the coordinating council for the Colorado Association of School Executives, and selection as planning principal for a new elementary school in Douglas County. Cheryl gained invaluable knowledge and skills about teaching, learning, and leadership through each of these challenging and rewarding professional experiences.

Cheryl lives with her husband, Wayne, in Castle Rock, Colorado, close to her two adult children, Jason and Megan, both of whom are teachers. She enjoys spending time with four grandchildren, reading, writing, and gardening in her spare time. She can be reached at (303) 504-9312, ext. 506, or via e-mail at cdunkle@leadandlearn.com.

# What Matters Most

*Teaching is the highest form of understanding.*
—Aristotle

**T**eachers are heroes, and teaching is a heroic act. You would be wasting your time if you tried to convince me otherwise. That might appear to be a rather bold, even brash and certainly biased statement to make, but after spending my entire adult life inside schools looking out at the broader community, I have come to realize that very lucky people get to hang out in schools. They are typically welcoming and happy places, filled with laughter, encouraging words, questions, answers, passion, and the personal power that learning can generate. This unique vantage point has allowed me to view the world from the innocent eyes of students, the trusting eyes of parents, and the compassionate eyes of teachers. Perhaps this perspective is the foundation for my far-reaching optimism and hope that America's future will be vibrant and vigorous once again.

I hold a deep conviction that the collective conversations necessary to strengthen our democratic society should include, as a main topic, what is happening in these special places called schools. For teaching and learning to flourish, educators, parents, community leaders, and policy makers must agree on what needs to be achieved here, what can be solved here, and what could be safely abandoned here. In essence, that is what the Common Core State Standards initiative challenges us to explore. Through careful examination of what educational expectations already exist in states across the nation, the authors of CCSS focus on clearer, fewer, and more rigorous standards in English language arts and mathematics so that our students have more opportunities available to them for college or career choices than ever before.

Teaching is, after all, the essential profession, the one that helps all other life decisions become a reality for students. More than ever before in our history, education will symbolize the difference between those who prosper in the new economy and those who will be left behind. This significant CCSS discussion can no longer endorse a system and its stakeholders as stewards of the status quo. The exercise of debating what to continue, what to change, and what to cast away will become of paramount importance in guiding these educational reform decisions. That is what CCSS invites us to address with the people who are closest to the problems and to the solutions—the teachers in our nation's classrooms.

It is obvious that truly incredible teaching and learning accomplishments are evident in thousands of classrooms across the nation, but the context can be subtle, sometimes intangible, and often difficult to describe even for a lifetime practitioner like myself. I keep asking, am I watching an individual with the passion, drive, inspiration, and desire to make a difference in the world; or am I observing a set of specialized, intricate, and learnable behaviors that are the result of thoughtful and thorough planning and preparation for the benefit of her learners? Is it her obvious respect for knowing what her students have, to then understand how to provide for what they need that is so evident in these dynamic and purposeful classrooms? Does great teaching occur as a result of the enduring qualities a teacher possesses within herself, or is it her ability to seamlessly respond to the daily situational influences that occur? These questions are critical to understanding, assessing, and ultimately replicating the complex work of quality teaching, and I will attempt to address some of them in the next few pages.

## ARE OUTSTANDING TEACHERS BORN OR MADE?

How do we identify what makes a great teacher? Is it truly an accident of birth that is only linked to genetic qualities or traits that cannot be taught, or can we discover certain common behaviors and required knowledge that are essential for teacher effectiveness? Is this the old nature versus nurture argument resurfacing in our dialogue?

I believe, like most, that there is no such entity as a born teacher who is naturally extraordinary. However, by nature, some individuals possess a combination of authentic personality traits that are conducive to excellence in teaching. Further, these qualities have been enriched by a lifetime of favorable nurturing. Nevertheless, in my opinion, even the most intuitive novice teacher benefits from a quality teacher education program initially and subsequent professional learning opportunities that hone her craft.

We regularly confuse teacher quality with teaching quality, as if the two were indistinguishable. We label teachers as caring, dedicated, positive, and fair, and these personal characteristics sometimes interfere with our ability to attribute certain principles of effectiveness to the extensive knowledge and skills they possess. Possibly, good teachers have certain dispositions that are more innate and intuitive, but my experience with great teachers and great teaching is that content knowledge, learning theory, instructional strategies, management techniques, assessment practices, and professionalism can be modeled and taught, refined and enhanced (National Board for Professional Teaching Standards, 2012; Council of Chief State School Officers, 2011).

As with most debates, the conjunction *and* is a better choice of words than the alternative, *either/or.* Great teaching is knowledge *and* wisdom; art *and* science, skills *and* dispositions; processes *and* products; content *and* pedagogy; and last, a journey *and* a destination. I believe that reestablishing these common understandings and agreements will remove many of the impediments to renewing and reframing the discussion about achieving equity and excellence in our public education system that CCSS encourages us to reinitiate. We want to get better at teaching and learning, and we can with focused attention and effort on the right work of reform.

## THE HEART OF THE MATTER

What does this all mean for beginning the daunting task of digging deep inside the Common Core State Standards to discover our next steps in educational reform? Hope for improving the future for America's students depends upon the degree to which passionate educators with a sense of moral purpose and a willingness to examine current practice have an opportunity to discuss realistic change with their colleagues. Teachers are indeed at the heart of the matter.

Teaching is difficult and sophisticated work, both intellectually and emotionally. What matters most for America's future is the acknowledgment that teacher excellence and teaching excellence are inseparable. Our compelling issues remain how to recognize who our exceptional teachers are, how to define the extraordinary things they do, and finally, how to replicate that effort in every classroom in America. Do you agree that this is no small task? I believe the impetus of the Common Core State Standards initiative offers the ideal starting point for these investigations and important dialogues to occur. The potential for this educational reform to push our thinking, propel us forward, and access our best ideas to apply to the lessons of research and experience is powerful. It represents a comprehensive and crucial response to the current educational issues we face as a nation.

I am not a Pollyanna who believes everything is perfect in paradise. I would not identify myself as a change agent if I thought no change is necessary. Now more than at any other time in our history, educators are asked to confront challenges that our current system is not designed or equipped to meet. Some parts are so badly broken that only radically new and potentially disruptive ideas will make a positive difference. These problems are not just dents in the system; they represent gaping holes. For example, the achievement gap between majority and minority populations, changing family structures, blatant poverty, reduced school budgets and resources, shortages of qualified teachers, and diversity issues such as access to quality English Language Learner and Special Education programs, just to name the short list, all require new attitudes and ventures that replace the ineffective and obsolete. Again, from my perspective, I see planning and preparing for implementing Common Core State Standards to be the heart of these discussions, helping to meet our collective goal of improving the quality of the learning experience for all of our students in all of our schools.

## THIS ISN'T KANSAS ANYMORE, TOTO

Everyone has an opinion about what is right with America's current educational system and what is wrong with it. Just ask, and citizens will eagerly espouse their personal tales of celebration or criticism, depending upon their individual experiences with teaching and learning. In one school you will hear parent complaints that there is too much homework and too little discipline, and that same school community will respond to a different set of parents who feel just the opposite; that there are not enough enrichment activities and the student conduct code is too strict and rigid. The big problem with this type of subjective assessment of quality is that it is grounded in private perception rather than public reality. In light of this realization, a valid question might be, aren't many of our current measurements of educational success or failure fact-free debates based upon an individual's unique response to an idea or belief?

It is our responsibility to offer accurate and researched information for the public and colleagues to consider. For example, if society accepts one prevalent belief that we all come into the world preset for success or failure with a permanent and limited capacity for growth and development, no amount of sustained work with common standards, common curricula, or common assessments currently proposed by CCSS advocates will change our results.

But think about this: Beliefs do matter. Why would we as educators work so hard in our schools to inspire, motivate, and encourage all adults and children to apply focused effort to learn new knowledge and skills if it is not possible for many to do so? Why would we structure opportunities for everyone to experience a challenging and rigorous curriculum if some students were not capable of engaging with complex concepts? And finally and most important, why would teachers and school leaders willingly accept responsibility for the disappointing outcomes on high-stakes assessments that we are currently witnessing with some groups of students, if they did not believe it is within their control to change those results? If we truly believe that no amount of hard work on causes will change the effects, why do we attempt with such passion to rewrite a positive ending to the achievement story for our youngsters who are struggling academically? Perhaps one answer is in understanding the importance of mindsets.

## MINDSETS

Mindsets constitute an uncomplicated yet profound idea that will help us address some of the important questions raised in the previous section. Stanford University psychologist Carol Dweck (2008), after decades of research on achievement and motivation, identifies two mindsets that play important roles in people's success. In one, the fixed mindset, people believe that their talents and abilities are fixed traits. They inherit a certain amount of intelligence, and nothing can be done to change their allotted quota. Many years of research have now shown that when people adopt the fixed mindset, it can significantly limit their perception of who they are as learners and what they can accomplish. They become overly concerned with publicly proving their talents and abilities and hiding their deficiencies and setbacks. Struggle and mistakes imply a predetermined lack of talent or ability. People with this mindset will actually pass up important opportunities to learn and grow if there is a risk of unmasking weaknesses.

In the other mindset, the growth mindset, people believe that their talents and abilities can be developed through passion, education, and persistence. For them, it is not about looking smart or grooming their image of intelligence. It is a commitment to getting better at something, to applying effective and focused effort, to taking informed risks, and to learning from honest feedback to improve the results. In a growth mindset, people create a love of learning and a resilience that is essential for great accomplishments. Virtually all successful people possess the growth mindset because it instills motivation, honors hard work, and rewards a positive attitude.

Dweck (2008) concludes that we need to foster in any learner, adult or student, a mindset of accomplishment that is attached to effective effort, not ability. We should encourage learners to stretch their potential and not limit natural eagerness or curiosity for discovery to preconceived notions of intelligence. My experience with learners and learning certainly confirms this conclusion.

The implications for fostering the growth mindset in our schools are dramatic for both students and adults. Some of our brightest students and most talented teachers avoid challenge, are uncomfortable with showing that effort is necessary to accomplish a goal, and wilt in the face of adversity because they are afraid of failing in front of their peers. In contrast, I have known resilient go-getters, who persist and achieve far more than anticipated when they work hard, request feedback, try again, and face obstacles head-on with a "can do" attitude. If we establish and nurture a learning community and culture that promotes risk-taking, supports inquiry, and rewards perseverance in learners, old and young, we are ready to confront the challenge of implementing Common Core State Standards in each of our schools. Learning how to learn and learning how to teach require the same diligence and focus, the same attitudes of bravery and efficacy; without a growth mindset, we will not move very far down the road toward educational reform.

## TEACHER LEADERSHIP

To be poised for success and benefit from the rich possibilities that the Common Core State Standards initiative brings to the work of transforming our system, we must consider what teaching as a profession requires to sustain itself, and most important, what supports our teachers' need to respond to these new performance demands. Reform needs pragmatism, humility, optimism, resourcefulness, persistence, cooperation, patience, and focus to garner results. It mandates an attitude from everyone involved that is committed to meeting difficult challenges with efficacy, energy, and expertise.

I know many extraordinary teachers. They are reflective about their work. They care deeply about their practice and their profession, and they explore provocative ideas thoughtfully and openly. They seek evidence-based solutions. They approach each day with a sense of urgency and moral purpose. They are authentic, innovative, and realistic. They thrive on challenge. They are catalysts for change and are resilient rather than resentful. Don't these qualities sound a lot like the characteristics of people who adopt a growth mindset? Isn't this the reason we should invite our best teachers to become the stars of the CCSS reform movement? This critical mass of practitioners who hold the same high standards for their students as they do for themselves, who have an extensive understanding of curriculum, instruction, and assessment, and who work hard for relevancy in their profession have the necessary qualifications to successfully launch this reform and create momentum to sustain it. Their invitation to join this effort and make productive contributions to it should already be printed and in the mail.

Sadly, in the face of increased public scrutiny, lack of resources, expanded demands to serve all students well, and unparalleled consequences for poor results, a few of our colleagues are confused, frustrated, and demoralized by the lack of trust and support we receive from some of our communities and stakeholders. The tendency for some teachers to become a bit resentful and defensive is a natural response to their perceptions of isolation and helplessness. To ensure the success of CCSS, we cannot ignore or forget about these disenfranchised and discouraged teachers. They must become the critical friends of this initiative so they begin to regain and renew their sense of hope for the future of education. Their feelings of significance and competence as they contribute to sustained and continuous improvement will apply the positive pressure that in fact elevates behavior to beliefs. Their invitation is ready and waiting as well.

We need passionate and bold teacher leaders to come forward, who live and work in the participating 46 states and Washington, D.C. where the CCSS have been adopted. Their guidance and unrelenting commitment to offer high-yield yet realistic solutions to the current problems that plague our educational system will move CCSS from idea to action faster than any other factor in improvement planning. In exchange for their bravery and initiative, they deserve everyone's support and respect, because without these visible and concrete assurances, we will reach an implementation impasse very quickly.

Douglas Reeves (2008) recognizes the potential power of teachers as leaders in any effort to transform our nation's schools. He offers some very insightful advice to publicly acknowledge the validity and significance of their contributions. He suggests

- Recognizing their excellence in accomplishing academic goals
- Emphasizing their freedom to use judgment, discretion, and authority
- Listening to and acting on their ideas
- Encouraging their innovation
- Providing feedback and coaching for their professional growth and development
- Valuing them as individuals
- Providing a sense of inclusion in their work
- Appreciating their diverse perspectives, ideas, and work styles
- Encouraging their full expression of ideas without fear of reprisal
- Listening to and fairly handling their complaints and concerns with dignity and respect

The commitment to the challenge of change must go deep into the hearts and minds of our best teachers for any substantive and sustained improvement to occur in our classrooms and schools. Accepting the role of change agent and understanding the content of change is a priority for all educators ready to champion the cause of CCSS. We must avoid at all costs the temptation to treat this initiative as another one-way mandate or another stand-alone education reform. Instead it should be viewed as an organic process; one that is complex, complicated, and multidimensional but also meaningful and doable with focused effort and a sense of efficacy. Because of its complexity, it must be viewed with a growth mindset. Implementation work must migrate from knowing to doing so that the potential impact and influence in school improvement begins and ends in the classroom with teachers assuming the headlining role as educational reformers.

## CHANGE IS SOMETIMES MESSY AND UNCOMFORTABLE

Typical and conventional educational change involves acquiring new materials and exploring new behaviors, practices, and policies that culminate in discovering and embracing new beliefs and understandings about our work. It implies continuous learning about and reevaluation of what we do and why we do it a certain way, and a realistic appraisal of how effective we are. It involves connecting peers to collaboratively view change as improvement, not just as behaviors that are different from the norm. It requires transparent data to inform the effort, capacity building to guide the effort, and shared leadership to direct, implement, and monitor the effort. The CCSS initiative requires the same careful and significant attention to following these principles of change.

Michael Fullan and colleagues (2005) contend that teacher leaders can be the drivers of reforms that create effective and enduring change and certain specific considerations that support success. They have identified eight forces for change leaders:

1. Engaging people's moral purposes about improving society through learning

2. Building capacity to increase people's collective power to move a system forward

3. Understanding the change process

4. Developing cultures for collaborative learning

5. Developing cultures of evaluation to sort out ideas that are promising from those that are not so promising

6. Focusing on shared leadership throughout the organization

7. Fostering coherence-making that involves alignment, connections, and clarity about the big picture

8. Cultivating tri-level development at the school and community, district, and state levels

The messiness and stress of change enters the work at a personal level when the potential loss of control and identity increases the lack of balance between the risk and the reward of any innovation. If we view ideas differently as a result of new learning, we consider how we can contribute in a different way as well. This fresh perspective sometimes requires us to shape and then reshape our actions to match the new understandings. If the pressure to take aim and hit ambitious targets prevails over our perceived ability to develop the new competencies necessary for success, inertia and even resistance sets in.

Any reform effort requires the overuse of a certain prefix. "Re" words have a tendency to creep into any conversation about how we move from tinkering with an existing system to transforming it to a new way of thinking. Consider, for example, the following brief list of 10 "re" words:

| | |
|---|---|
| Reform | Reframe |
| Rethink | Revisit |
| Renew | Retrain |
| Regain | Reinvent |
| Refocus | Reestablish |

These verbs should guide our initial conversations about the current state of our educational system, but they should not inhibit our ability to think beyond what already exists to the desired state of what public education can become. This is what the dynamics of change and CCSS demand of us.

## WHAT HAPPENS NEXT WITH CCSS REFORM?

If we agree that teachers are the key players in ensuring that any change initiative enters the classroom, how do we create the conditions necessary for them to share their enthusiasm and concerns for how CCSS will impact their work with students? How do we encourage open and honest dialogue about the challenges and the opportunities of viewing CCSS as the starting point for educational reform? Consider the following recommendations:

- Be proactive and take ownership for the process of designing a focused CCSS transition plan and a comprehensive implementation plan that address the scope of the work, realistic timelines, key deliverables, and ongoing quality measurements to monitor both plans.
- Make CCSS the focus of any future discussions about curriculum, instruction, and assessment decisions.
- Build awareness and understanding of the tenets of CCSS to identify which instructional practices will remain the same and which will need modification.
- Create a gap analysis process that compares existing standards, curriculum, and assessments with CCSS.
- Take inventory of what professional learning will be necessary to build the instructional capacity of teachers to meet the challenges of CCSS.
- Evaluate the targets of "fewer, clearer, and higher" standards in your current context.
- Discuss the CCSS benefits of efficiency of scale, equity, and uniformity.
- Begin to look at resources and materials that align with cross-disciplinary and project-based learning.
- Develop authentic performance tasks that engage learners with the new standards.
- Emphasize informational writing as a thinking tool in all content areas.
- Create common formative assessments to provide ongoing monitoring of student progress in English language arts and mathematics at each level.

- Acknowledge CCSS as an opportunity to renew professionalism and regain respect for teaching and learning.

## FROM COMMON SENSE TO COMMON PRACTICE IN TEACHER LEADERSHIP

If "knowing how" were enough to motivate us to make positive change in our practices, then we would all be rich and thin, right? For example, everyone "knows" that it is unhealthy to be overweight, and yet 64% of Americans are, and an amazing 30% are technically obese according to the Centers for Disease Control and Prevention (http://www.cdc.org). Ask any group of savvy adults for suggestions on how to lose a few pounds and they will respond with some insightful and obvious dieting advice like "Eat less and exercise more." Typically, sound ideas are not profound or complicated. They always represent common sense, but they do not necessarily invoke common practice. If it were common practice to eat less and exercise more, then we would not be dealing with the health risks and costs associated with an overweight society.

Notice that the last statement contains an "if . . . then" relationship or hypothesis, which is a prediction about what you might expect to see happen as a result of a decision, a behavior, or a belief. With colleagues at the Leadership and Learning Center, the heart of many of our conversations involves a powerful concept called antecedents of excellence. It is an educational "if . . . then" exercise to explain the success of school improvement and systemic reform efforts. Douglas Reeves proposes in part that antecedents are structures and conditions that precede, anticipate, or predict excellence in performance. They are precursors to high student achievement, success in implementing a new program or strategy, or completing authentic tasks with focus and precision. They are predictors of positive results that associate a cause with an effect (Reeves, 2006).

Why don't we, as educators, consistently do what we know makes good sense? If we identify our goal and understand through knowledge and experience how to reach the goal, why do we sometimes waver in our pursuit of it? Oftentimes, the challenge is difficult, like dieting, and requires participants to modify their behavior through the hard work of changing habits. Sometimes the idea is controversial and untested and requires new thinking about the way we currently behave. Other times the decision is politically divisive and polarizes people's belief about the larger issues. Common Core State Standards is a commonsense reform initiative, but without focused energy and diligent effort on the part of educators, parents, community leaders, and policy makers, its potential to become common practice is in constant jeopardy.

As a summary to this chapter about teaching quality, teacher leadership, and school reform efforts, I submit for your consideration some "if . . . then" statements that might generate some logical and commonsense conversations that will indeed translate into common practices in our classrooms and schools.

- If America's social and economic future depends upon our students receiving a world-class education, then teacher and school leaders must offer their energy and expertise to suggest how to close the achievement gap for all students.
- If the educational status quo is no longer adequate to ensure our nation's global competitiveness, then the achievement bar must be raised for all students.
- If teacher leadership is at the heart of any reform, then we must encourage our extraordinary teachers to become involved and substantively contribute to the successful implementation of CCSS.
- If reality in a classroom is sometimes misrepresented, then we must share accurate data with our stakeholders to debunk the myths of our work.
- If the components of an educational system are aligned, focused, and consistent, then common agreements about curriculum, instruction, and assessment are easier to reach.
- If CCSS comprehensively states what students need to know and be able to do for college and career readiness, then we need to conduct a gap analysis to ascertain what already exists that is useful to the effort and what needs to change, be created, or be eliminated.
- If we believe that any change or reform effort is challenging, then we must be thoughtful about what is necessary to support the people involved who are the agents of the change.

So those are my thoughts on the importance of engaging invested teachers in the conversation about CCSS implementation considerations, and it ends my cheerleading for the home team. The reality is that 46 states and Washington, D.C., are already in the "big" game and need our full attention and support to avoid the potential fits and starts of any change or reform effort.

Three constant features are included at the end of each chapter in this book to foster further professional conversations. The first is a leadership strategy that helps define a logical plan to sequence and prioritize some ideas for action. Do this now, do this next, and do this later is similar to the tried and true protocol of examining what to keep, what to amend, and what to abandon when "weeding the garden" of too many conflicting initiatives that vie for time, resources, and focus. The second summary section lists key ideas mentioned in the chapter that could serve as discussion points in a professional learning community meeting or other forum. The final inclusion identifies some focused and provocative questions to frame a book study or perhaps some other type of critical inquiry to move this reform forward.

## DO THIS NOW, DO THIS NEXT, AND DO THIS LATER

### Now . . .

Communicate, communicate, and communicate some more about the direct implications CCSS will have for districts, schools, and classrooms.

Focus on the direct benefits and goals of CCSS to strengthen the broad-based educator support for the initiative.

Invite a motivated, creative, and knowledgeable team who will take ownership for building the CCSS vision and for proactively designing a transition plan in your system from the current state of education to the desired state.

### Next . . .

Make quality online resources accessible to investigate what other early adopting states have discovered about CCSS implementation. Recommendations are New York; Indiana; Utah; Ohio; Massachusetts; California; Washington, D.C.; Delaware; and Illinois.

Begin the cross-walking task of conducting a gap and overlap analysis of existing standards, curriculum, and assessments, comparing them with the new CCSS to determine what changes in practice are necessary and what will remain unchanged in current policy.

Determine an entry point for CCSS to be introduced into your system. Most recommend beginning with a foundational primary grade level, such as kindergarten through second grade. Check out the exemplary Cleveland Metro plan for ideas.

### Later . . .

Get into the details about how the transition to CCSS will look, how it will be accomplished, and how CCSS will work within the current system.

Begin a collaborative analysis of student work samples to compare with the exemplars contained in the CCSS appendices as another experience with the range of rigor that currently exists.

Create partnerships with professional organizations and state groups that have knowledge of the transition plans available in your state to share and distribute information, resources, and experience.

## KEY IDEAS FOR CHAPTER 1

→ Schools are dynamic places because teaching and learning is an active and engaging process.

→ Hope for improving the future for America's students depends upon the degree to which educators with a sense of moral purpose and a willingness to examine current practice have an opportunity to discuss realistic change with their colleagues.

→ Teaching is very complex intellectual and emotional work, and identifying who our excellent teachers are and our ability to describe precisely and consistently what they do is at the heart of school reform.

→ We must embrace the concept of a growth mindset for adults and students to persevere in meeting the challenge of learning more at deeper and more complex levels of understanding.

→ If systemic reform does not positively impact the students in the classroom, then clearly there is no reform.

→ Change is a challenging process that requires energy, ideas, commitment, and ownership from everyone in the organization.

## QUESTIONS TO CONTINUE THIS DISCUSSION

☑ How do we formalize the process of identifying and celebrating the work of great teachers and great teaching that translates into significant learning for our students?

☑ How do we present the concept of a growth mindset to teachers and students to cultivate the attitude that sustained and focused effort is the key to learning challenging new material and testing new ideas?

☑ How do we communicate the required sense of urgency so that our best teacher leaders are exploring and evaluating the potential implications of CCSS in the context of real classrooms and real schools to guide the initiative forward?

☑ What will success look like once CCSS is initially embedded into every educational reform conversation and finally into every classroom in America?

☑ How can we collectively rewrite the ending to the achievement success story for all of our students?

# Leading With Roots and Wings

2

*To accomplish great things*
*We must not only act,*
*But also dream,*
*Not only plan,*
*But also believe.*

—Anatole France

**W**e can agree that classroom teachers carry the greatest responsibility for improving student learning and are the most important determinants in school-based student success. Extensive research supports this logical conclusion and so does common sense.

Teachers are accountable for organizing engaging standards-based learning activities, communicating rigorous curricular goals, assessing for accurate performance results, and differentiating instruction in response to those results.

However, an essential consideration in any substantive educational reform is the realization that we need effective schools, not just isolated effective classrooms, to ensure that the highest quality of teaching and learning is delivered to all students. There is a significant diminished return on systemic improvement efforts if students move from an outstanding teacher to a mediocre or even chronically ineffective one the very next school year. Several research studies assert that the long-term impact of being placed with a poor-performing teacher can have profoundly negative cumulative effects on the achievement of students over time (Hattie, 2009). We must do better for the sake of all of our children, and connecting robust understandings about school leadership to deliberate adult actions is paramount in avoiding depressed achievement results for any student, but especially for those whose learning needs are most acute.

I believe, as many do, that America's best schools are in fact among the best in the world. They prepare and produce outstanding students who have the knowledge, skills, and attitudes necessary to accomplish whatever they desire in life. Other schools are succeeding, often under very difficult circumstances, in reaching most of their students, but the widespread national concern is that far too many schools are marginal at best and are failing to provide opportunities for an excellent educational experience for every one of their students. At a recent celebration of Blue Ribbon Schools, Secretary of Education Arne Duncan acknowledged the important role that principals play in creating the conditions under which teachers can succeed in the classroom. "We have no good schools in this country without good principals, and, I assure you, we have no great schools without great principals," he said (jreeves, 2010). My experience confirms his statement.

What do great principals believe about teaching and learning, and what do great principals do as a result of those beliefs?

## CONSIDER THIS SCENARIO

The proposal was finished. Ellen Patterson rubbed her gritty eyes and scooted slowly away from her computer. Twenty pages exposing her professional head and heart were now warm from the printer and lying neatly on her desk. Her vision for re-creating the lowest performing school in her district appeared officially in black and white and was now a living, breathing document for people to critique, consider, and criticize. Ellen's quiet, private thoughts and reflections would now be topics for public conversations.

In draft after draft and revision after revision, Ellen wrote from a leader's soul to convey a powerful description of the perfect school with the eloquence, substance, insight, and savvy of her professional idols. The highlighted and somewhat tattered copies of books by Barth, Boyer, Covey, Reeves, Fullan, Haycock, Darling-Hammond, Schmoker, Senge, Marzano, and Hattie, just to name a few, were strewn across her overflowing shelf and evidenced the power and influence of these authors on Ellen's current thinking about school leadership and its impact on quality teaching and learning. This research-based perspective, coupled with her craft knowledge and 28 years of successful experience as a teacher and principal, were the legitimate credentials for embarking on this challenging, consuming, and courageous journey of turning around a marginal school. Ellen was proud of the final copy and knew it represented her best effort at communicating her passionate beliefs about rebuilding a dream school where children and adults, short and tall, enthusiastic and cautious, would assemble to become a confident, competent, responsible, and resourceful community of learners.

But did her words share with conviction that this reconstituted school would model the beliefs that every child has the right to a worthwhile and valuable educational experience; that this learning community would be held to the very highest academic and behavioral standards; and that, most important, in this building, all children would learn and succeed? Would those 28 years in education suffice as worthy qualifications for accepting this professional challenge? Would the extensive reading, research, and reflection she had completed indicate the degree of her commitment and dedication toward this responsibility? Did she have the time and talent to spend on behalf of these students? Would the passion of Ellen's personal vision ignite a fire within others to join with her, sleeves rolled up, to create a Common Core State Standards prototype school? Doubts began to surface and Ellen's once buoyed confidence level seemed to spring a leak when these questions crept into her thoughts. But after some positive self-talk, she realized she was as prepared as she would ever be to pursue this leadership opportunity. She would offer her framework for considering a "standards at the start" school and hope that her dedication to a dream would affect change in the world.

What do you notice about this fictional representation of a principal's desire to be the catalyst for educational change? There are no quick fixes or formulas mentioned for accomplishing the complicated goals that Ellen recounts. The path she proposes to follow to improve a failing school is strewn with obstacles, unresolved questions, and difficult policy choices for all stakeholders to consider in the school reform process. But if there is a national imperative to fix what is broken in our marginal schools, then there is also a national imperative to support school leaders in their attempts to translate an educational vision into a reality that results in successful learning for all students.

## VARIATIONS ON THE LEADERSHIP THEME

The updated Interstate Leaders Licensure Consortium Educational Leadership Policy Standards reissued in December 2008 by the Council of Chief State School Officers (CCSSO) in collaboration with the National Policy Board on Educational Administration (NPBEA) have provided a framework for all 50 states to either adopt or adapt six recommended standards of effective leadership practices (CCSSO, 2008). Each standard is followed by the specific functions of leadership required to meet the standard. This extensive list provides a starting point in defining what school leaders need to know and be able to do to lead highly effective schools.

Six seems to be the magic number for leadership standards since the National Association of Elementary School Principals (NAESP; 2009) also mentions six strategies for effective leadership practice. My bias is that they are clearly written, comprehensive, and not bound to a K–5 perspective. They can be applied appropriately at a middle or high school level as well.

If we examine the aggregate message of these standards more closely in the context of our work with students and adults, we see a relentless focus on learning as the perpetual theme. We can distill both sets of statements into four priorities for assessing effective school leadership. How well leaders accomplish the following challenges determines how successful they will be in leading learning communities (Boyer, 1995). They must

- Connect people to create a shared vision of an inclusive and purposeful learning community
- Connect the structures of curriculum, instruction, and assessment to create rigorous standards-based academic coherence
- Connect classrooms to practices and programs that enrich a high-performance culture for learning
- Connect learning to life, building the capacity of everyone to define the moral and ethical dimensions of high expectations for behavior and achievement

## THE WINGS OF VISION

Extensive research-based study reveals that effective school leaders, first and foremost, are people-builders (Reeves, 2006). They initiate and maintain a culture that is respectful of relationships and advocates for the integrity of diverse ideas and opinions. School leaders think deeply about how to stimulate thoughtful and reflective discussions that result in establishing a shared and common vision about the moral purpose of schooling. Leading by example, they display behaviors that honor the broader view, that acknowledge different perspectives, and that deliberately shape and guide this valuable collaboration through dialogue. They help build the capacity of the adults to see the limitless possibilities generated by bold thinking and courageous action.

If you are reading the pages of this chapter, you have already indicated a strong desire to contribute as a school leader to the creation of this positive learning environment and to watching with vigilance as it transforms the lives of children. In order to participate in this grand endeavor you must be a planner, a doer, an inspirer, a believer, and most of all, a visionary.

The term *vision* is one of the most frequently used educational buzzwords of our time. Everyone is searching for the value-laden words that can communicate a dream to their stakeholders. It typically is typed in a dramatic and colorful font, mounted as a glossy poster, and hung on a predominant office wall. But a vision is much more than window dressing or the fad of the week. It is the basis and support for clarifying our purpose; it points us in the right direction and motivates us to perform beyond our resources and even our potential. It represents the wings of an organization and is an indispensable, shared, and common picture of what the future can and should be.

Some declare a school vision is an "internal compass." Others call it a dream or the distance between the real and the ideal. Peter Senge, in his book *The Fifth Discipline: The Art and Practice of the Learning Organization*, describes vision as a "shared picture of the future we seek to create" (1990). He emphasizes that vision is not an idea but a powerful force that is necessary to focus and energize our learning. Jim Collins, a current organizational researcher and writer, states, "There is a very big difference between being an organization with a vision statement and becoming a truly visionary organization. The difference lies in creating alignment to preserve an organization's core values, to reinforce its purpose, and to stimulate continued progress towards its aspirations" (2001). Viktor Frankl, a holocaust survivor, revered vision as "the ability to see beyond our present reality, to create, to invent what does not exist, to become what we not yet are" (2006). He credited the ability to be a visionary with preserving and extending life during the world's most dehumanizing time and place, World War II in the Nazi concentration camps.

A visionary educator passionately believes that she can make a dramatic difference in the lives of children. She believes she can change the future and creates mental images of what the ideal school looks like, sounds like, and feels like. Then through quiet persuasion or loud cheerleading, she invites others into her dream.

Reaching a common agreement on the shared language and meaning of a vision requires extensive dialogue among stakeholders. Individuals who have joined a learning community based upon a clearly articulated vision must reinforce the following essential questions:

- Why do we exist? For what purpose are we creating this learning community?
- What do we stand for? What are our unwavering beliefs about students, teaching, and learning?

- What do we want to accomplish with our students?
- How will we measure success?
- How will we personally and professionally contribute to the vision through the investment of time and talents?

A vision should not represent a compromise of personal beliefs. It requires that we all revisit our core values, and that is not a quick or surface exercise. The vision statement challenges and stretches, but it is not in conflict with individual values. It should connect and bond a community by outlining common aspirations and a caring commitment to what is collectively agreed upon as the right way to do the right things for students. Once this is established, a compelling shared vision provides the inner and outer standards of excellence: what we need, what we do not need, and what is considered non-negotiable. It is this combined synergy of the group that evokes pride, purpose, passion, and identity. Stephen Covey (1990) states that a shared vision represents" finding true north." The discussions and conversations that accompany these questions offer the guideposts to locate that direction and stay on course. They give us sustained energy to transform and transcend the legacy we leave for generations to come.

Vision statements are not short, sharp, or snappy marketing phrases. The great ones represent the heartfelt consensus on the core values about teaching, learning, and leadership that matter in a school community and direct the new actions that are necessary to translate the rhetoric into results.

These deeply held beliefs provide the contextual big picture for the organization and act as the sort and select filters for what the institution is seeking to accomplish. They form the basis for how learning priorities are determined and discriminate between the essential and nonessential work. This leads us to explore the roots of educational leadership: coherence between the moral purpose and the adult decisions and actions that drive the changes and reforms necessary to reach their vision.

## THE ROOTS OF COHERENCE

If vision represents the wings of a learning community, then the roots are the obvious connections among the systems and structures, practices, and programs that provide the infrastructure or operating system for effective teaching and learning. The deliberate realignment of rigorous content standards to challenging curricula, engaging instructional strategies, and authentic assessments is the primary task of coherence making for teachers. For school leaders, coherence making demands that we closely reexamine each unique aspect of school policies and procedures to evaluate which models need to be redesigned and which must be created to directly contribute to student and adult learning success. For both teachers and principals, the roots of coherence are planted firmly in the spirit of innovation and creativity to discover the pieces of the system that no longer realistically fit together. Coherence making enlarges our sense of possibilities and opportunities and ensures that we are utilizing personal connections and relationships to inform our professional judgment and decisions. It is exciting and stimulating work.

As Daniel Pink (2009) proposes in his thoughtful book on motivation, *Drive: The Surprising Truth About What Motivates Us*, Type I individuals and organizations identify with the concepts of autonomy, mastery, and purpose. They respond to encouragement better than praise, they work for intrinsic satisfaction rather than external rewards, and they value significant work and the opportunity to collaborate with colleagues to contribute to the greater good. Pink elaborates in his list, Carrots and Sticks: The Seven Deadly Flaws:

1. They can extinguish intrinsic motivation.
2. They can diminish performance.
3. They can crush creativity.
4. They can crowd out good behavior.
5. They can encourage cheating, shortcuts, and unethical behavior.
6. They can become addictive.
7. They can foster short-term thinking.

I have very similar beliefs as a result of my affiliation with outstanding educators. My work as a planning principal opening a new district elementary school allowed me to choose 10 incredibly high-performing Type I staff members who gave form, structure, and conceptual integrity to my ideas and vision of what a successful learning environment would embody. They exemplified all of the positive descriptors in Pink's book and were a professional learning community before the current term was even coined.

We lovingly called the intense and focused planning sessions our Tuesday night revival meetings. They were as emotionally charged, intellectually stimulating, and spiritually invigorating as any evangelical gathering. The team received no compensation for their involvement, yet spent hours and hours over the course of nine months dreaming, defining, designing, and developing the perfect school for our community. They each assumed responsibility for becoming an expert in one aspect of effective teaching practice and shared their research and recommendations with the group. Our strategic plan represented months of extended discussions reflecting and refining and then was drafted into a brilliantly written document in 20 minutes. It represented the heart and soul of our proposal and was a source of immense pride.

My leadership experience with that core team confirms my conviction that any significant initiative needs special nurturing so that the essential people involved have ample opportunities to learn together, plan together, and celebrate together. The delight and the difficulty with the daunting task of creating anything new in education is that we are rarely required or requested to think about our craft and the "why" of our work. Time for research and reexamination is a luxury for most professionals, and in light of our current reform challenges, we need to ensure that allocated time for these importance dialogues about purpose and practice is the rule rather than the exception.

The new roots, the current foundational elements of our mandate to improve teaching and learning, rest with the recently adopted Common Core State Standards. Our most pressing responsibility as school leaders is to gather the "right people on the bus" (Collins, 2001) to create a consistent understanding, an informed acceptance, and a dedicated commitment to the strategic implementation of CCSS. It requires that we reconnect our vision of shared leadership and purpose with our daily actions and practices. Our future as school leaders for at least the next decade will involve making sense of the implications that the CCSS initiative will have on our work with students and how we are going to leave a positive imprint on the educational landscape that will accompany this broad-based reform.

School leaders serve as the critical scaffold between any proposed educational initiative and the genuine difference that change potentially makes on the quality of teaching and learning in a building. They define the mission, manage the plan, and promote the climate to get the work accomplished. By setting a clear and defensible course that wins cooperation from everyone, by developing the people's capacity to successfully implement the reform through support and training, and by redesigning the system to accommodate a stronger culture, different structures, and collaborative processes, a leader can create the professional community that raises the bar on standards for student learning. That effort should mirror the Tuesday night revival meetings with eagerness, enthusiasm, and engagement based upon rich conversations rather than stand-and-deliver presentations.

Douglas Reeves (2011), in a recent book, *Finding Your Leadership Focus: What Matters Most for Student Results,* describes an affliction prevalent in schools today. It is labeled the Law of Initiative Fatigue and has dramatic implications for our work with CCSS implementation. He highlights the inverse relationship between too many programs piled on top of one another and the measure of effectiveness of each one independently. More is definitely not better in this case. Especially in the context of diminished resources of time, funding, and emotional energy, this phenomenon creates feelings of stress and frustration in those who are responsible for implementing the sometimes disconnected and lengthy laundry list of system priorities. Sensitive school leaders must be responsive to the cumulative effect that adding the new or changing the old has on the reality of overload and fragmentation on classroom teachers. Attitudes and performance suffer as a result of a lack of focus and a diminished sense of efficacy in meeting the competing demands of change. Change generates emotional reactions of vitality and vigor on the positive side, but also feelings of fear, loss, and sometimes panic that can debilitate people on the other.

Leaders must protect Common Core State Standards from appearing in the discard pile of these competing initiatives and ensure that we do not fatigue when thinking about the enormity of this reform on our profession. The new direction of CCSS should be considered the metaphorical basket that contains many of the current thoughts and beliefs, programs, and practices that benefit teaching and learning. One of our first leadership challenges in promoting this initiative will be to locate and preserve time to collaborate with our teams to determine what will not change in our work—to revisit and reestablish the wings and roots of our organization.

## FROM COMMON SENSE TO COMMON PRACTICE IN SCHOOL LEADERSHIP

It was the best of times, it was the worst of times, it was the age of wisdom, it was the age of foolishness, it was the epoch of belief, it was the epoch of incredulity, it was the season of Light, it was the season of Darkness, it was the spring of hope, it was the winter of despair, we had everything before us, we had nothing before us, we were all going direct to heaven, we were all going direct the other way—in short, the period was so far like the present period, that some of its noisiest authorities insisted on its being received, for good or for evil, in the superlative degree of comparison only.

—Charles Dickens, *A Tale of Two Cities* (1859)

Brilliant words often have relevance in unusual contexts and situations that have nothing to do with the original writing. This quote is one of the most famous openings to any published piece of literature in the world and describes vast extremes and contradictions that occurred during the French Revolution. Depending upon your perspective, this sentiment could be shared today in our current discussions about the need for educational reform. Maybe some of us think of this challenge as a different type of revolution. It certainly represents transformation and change.

These are truly unsettled times for leadership in teaching and learning. Some who have been active participants in the enterprise for decades see unpredictable environments, chaotic conditions, and vulnerable relationships between reformers and realists. Others view these times as exciting opportunities to openly look at new ideas to solve the current equity and excellence problems in education. After extensive study in researching for this book, I tend to side with colleagues who welcome the prospect of reinvesting in our profession in a meaningful way.

This will not be easy or uncomplicated work. There can be no ambiguity or hedging on our part. The time for facing facts about student achievement without a defensive posture is here. My two heroes in the field of aggressive educational reform, Douglas Reeves and Michael Fullan, agree that collective inquiry and commitment to action will cause and sustain positive change in teaching and learning effectiveness. Both offer invaluable counsel on how to create systemic interventions that lead to fundamental transformations in our efforts to educate all of our students to high levels.

Reeves (2006) has created a very plausible leadership and learning framework (see Exhibit 2.1) that helps us make powerful connections between the antecedents of excellence or productive adult actions in a system and the achievement results that students realize. These relationships form four categories of schools that stimulate conversations about the influence our behavior has on school reform initiatives.

| | |
|---|---|
| **Lucky**<br><br>High results, low understanding of antecedents<br><br>Replication of success unlikely | **Leading**<br><br>High results, high understanding of antecedents<br><br>Replication of success likely |
| **Losing**<br><br>Low results, low understanding of antecedents<br><br>Replication of mistakes likely | **Learning**<br><br>Low results, high understanding of antecedents<br><br>Replication of mistakes unlikely |

*Achievement of Results* (vertical axis label)

**Understanding of the Antecedents of Excellence**

**Exhibit 2.1**     Leadership and Learning Matrix

*Source:* Reeves (2006). Used with permission.

His research also identifies and dispels five myths that interfere with and delay action for improvement:

- Myth No. 1: People are happy doing what they are doing now. Teachers in unsuccessful schools would rather continue to be unsuccessful than engage in alternative practices that might lead to student success.
- Myth No. 2: People resist change because of irrational fear.
- Myth No. 3: You can't make significant changes until you get buy-in from everybody.
- Myth No. 4: You must have perfect research to support a proposed change.
- Myth No. 5: The risk of change is so great that you must wait until you have things perfectly organized before implementing change efforts.

Action-oriented leadership follows the practices of reviewing data, making midcourse corrections based on that data, and implementing decisions that have the greatest points of systemic leverage. Dr. Reeves pushes us to make perpetual learning for all adults and students our unwavering responsibility and accountability target.

Michael Fullan (2001) supports leadership considerations of high-performance learning cultures in creating a readiness for the changes necessary to successfully implement any initiative. All members of the school community share beliefs about ability and achievement, efficacy and effort, and power and control, and these beliefs are directly connected to the structures of relationships, the learning culture, and the policies and procedures inherent in the school.

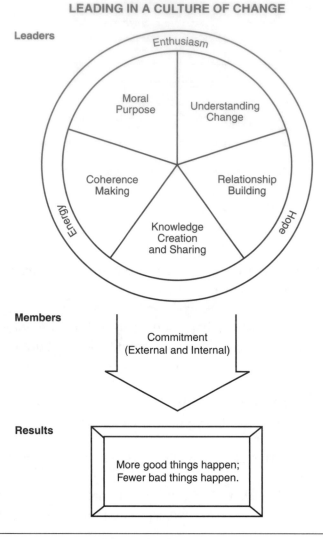

**Exhibit 2.2**    Framework for Leadership

*Source:* Fullan (2001).

Concepts such as collaboration and distributed accountability have real relevance and meaning for establishing a learning team's ability to manage the requirements of an educational reform. A school clearly focused on teaching and learning success generates energy that propels students, teachers, and parents into a cycle of ever-higher expectations and ultimately, performance. School leaders need to capitalize on this powerful attribute of change. Fullan's model of a framework for leadership (see Exhibit 2.2) emphasizes that turning information into knowledge is a social process that requires time and persistence.

The Common Core State Standards initiative challenges school leaders to become proficient systems thinkers and change agents. CCSS defines what academic success looks like, but local educators will need to personalize that view by translating those standards and expectations into the unique context of each individual district and school. We will be asked to review and reevaluate every program, policy, and procedure to assess its alignment with the new standards. To hold high standards for learning for every student and adult requires a vision that stimulates thought and coherence that establishes an instructional core. Schools that thrive in this new paradigm of rigor will need leaders who nurture both the roots and wings of their organization.

## DO THIS NOW, DO THIS NEXT, AND DO THIS LATER

### Now . . .

Publish a flexible transition framework that reinforces some of the considerations about what will shift during the implementation of CCSS.

Protect the focus on CCSS and suspend all new initiatives that could potentially divert attention from this comprehensive implementation goal.

Begin offering hands-on learning sessions for professionals to explore alignments in curriculum, instruction, and assessments to identify learning targets, to ask relevant questions, and to work through the perceived hurdles to implementation with peers.

### Next . . .

Begin investigating the PARCC (http://www.parcconline.org/) and SBAC (http://www.k12.wa.us/smarter/) websites to locate resources that assist with CCSS implementation efforts and provide current information about the proposed assessment blueprints.

Provide opportunities for grade-level and content-area teams of teachers to meet to revisit the CCSS documents and discuss implications for their work with the new standards.

In collaboration with others, go deeper in creating the transition roadmap to align it with the roots and wings of leading the CCSS implementation effort.

### Later . . .

Begin rethinking structures such as staffing, scheduling, curriculum course design, instructional resources, common formative assessments, and ways to promote professional dialogue to advance the CCSS work.

Openly discuss the challenges that will need to be overcome to ensure that the momentum for CCSS continues.

Read the publication *On the Road to Implementation: Achieving the Promise of the Common Core State Standards* (Achieve, Inc., 2010) to explore comprehensive ideas about implementation planning and preparation.

## KEY IDEAS FOR CHAPTER 2

→ A leader's dilemma is discovering how to cultivate and sustain student and adult learning in conditions of complex and rapid change.

→ Acting with intention to make a positive difference in the world defines the elements of our moral purpose, personal values, and professional priorities as school leaders.

→ Building the capacity of people to understand and endorse change is the first leadership implication in educational reform efforts like CCSS.

→ The effective school leader considers the influence of people before the impact of programs.

→ Powerful visions are the wings of an organization that represents the common agreements and compelling goals shared by all.

→ The roots of a system are the foundational connections made between a set of principles and the coherence of those ideas to daily practice.

## QUESTIONS TO CONTINUE THIS DISCUSSION

☑ How do our leadership skills support everyone's involvement in the vital conversations about what is the moral purpose for our work in schools?

☑ How do our learning communities ensure that all of the elements of our vision—the wings of our organization—are visible and evident in our language, our behavior, and most important our commitment to and decisions about quality teaching and learning?

☑ How do we consistently examine the coherence—the roots—between what we believe about student and adult learning and the existing practices and programs that support the implementation of those beliefs?

☑ How do school leaders foster changes that realign and refine the connections between a school reform initiative such as CCSS and the actions in the classroom where students feel the direct impact of the change?

☑ How does the concept of initiative fatigue interfere with our work with CCSS implementation?

☑ What are some antecedents of excellence that are evident in your work with students?

# The Promises and Possibilities of Common Core State Standards

*If we cannot learn wisdom from experience,
it is hard to say where it is to be found.*

—George Washington

The 2011–2012 school year represents the formal launch of the Common Core State Standards initiative in many of the adopting states and territories. It is the source of much angst and hand-wringing but also of great anticipation and excitement to discuss what the educational fuss is all about. Not since 1983 and the release of *A Nation at Risk* have we had such powerful and passionate discussions about teaching and learning in America. I believe the reason for some of this emotional intensity in our conversations could be that we are still talking about relatively the same issues that were concerning us in 1983. Twenty-eight years of asking:

- Are we making a significant difference in the lives of our students?
- Are we doing all we can to help every student excel in learning and be prepared for the next step in life?
- Is there more to understand about our work?
- How do we learn to do more and do it more effectively and efficiently?
- Is what is required of us, as educators, humanly possible?

As a legitimate introduction to a discussion about the merits of implementing the Common Core State Standards initiative and the potential obstacles, let's reflect candidly and with an open mind about these prophetic words that were written in 1983.

## ARE WE STILL A NATION AT RISK?

All, regardless of race or class or economic status, are entitled to a fair chance and to the tools for developing their individual powers of mind and spirit to the utmost. This promise means that all children by virtue of their own efforts, competently guided, can hope to attain the mature and informed judgment needed to secure gainful employment, and to manage their own lives, thereby serving not only their own interests but also the progress of society itself. (National Commission on Excellence in Education, 1983)

"Our Nation is at risk. Our once unchallenged preeminence in commerce, industry, science, and technological innovation is being overtaken by competitors throughout the world. This report is concerned with only one of the many causes and dimensions of the problem, but it is the one that undergirds American prosperity, security, and civility. We report to the American people that while we can take justifiable pride in what our schools and colleges have historically accomplished and contributed to the United States and the well-being of its people, the educational foundations of our society are presently being eroded by a rising tide of mediocrity that threatens our very future as a Nation and a people. What was unimaginable a generation ago has begun to occur—others are matching and surpassing our educational attainments.

If an unfriendly foreign power had attempted to impose on America the mediocre educational performance that exists today, we might well have viewed it as an act of war. As it stands, we have allowed this to happen to ourselves. We have even squandered the gains in student achievement made in the wake of the Sputnik challenge. Moreover, we have dismantled essential support systems that helped make those gains possible. We have, in effect, been committing an act of unthinking, unilateral educational disarmament.

Our society and its educational institutions seem to have lost sight of the basic purposes of schooling, and of the high expectations and disciplined effort needed to attain them.

> This report, the result of 18 months of study, seeks to generate reform of our educational system in fundamental ways and to renew the Nation's commitment to schools and colleges of high quality throughout the length and breadth of our land.
>
> That we have compromised this commitment is, upon reflection, hardly surprising, given the multitude of often conflicting demands we have placed on our Nation's schools and colleges. They are routinely called on to provide solutions to personal, social, and political problems that the home and other institutions either will not or cannot resolve. We must understand that these demands on our schools and colleges often exact an educational cost as well as a financial one. We are confident that the American people, properly informed, will do what is right for their children and for the generations to come." (National Commission on Excellence in Education, 1983)

Yes, we are still at risk. Actually, many educational experts believe that we have lost significant ground in our battle against mediocrity since 1983. My first principalship began in that same year, and the realization that we are still addressing similar concerns about educational equity and excellence 28 years later is very disconcerting to me. The sense of urgency that was conveyed in the *Nation At Risk* report has done little to mobilize us to find solutions to the myriad of challenges we faced then and continue to face now in achieving educational quality for all of our students.

There is hope and better news. We have a new transparency about our problems as a result of the immense efforts to collect student performance data for No Child Left Behind (NCLB) and other accountability mandates. Some say we are "data rich but information poor." My response is that we are information rich but implementation wary. We are very capable of identifying and defining our difficulties; we know the daunting scope of our problems; we even are aware of some very logical solutions to them. Our barrier to change is that we do not push hard enough when we have these rare opportunities to reboot our system to determine what is essential for high performance in teaching and learning. More than 90% of our states and territories have taken that first step to explore the reform prospects by voluntarily adopting the Common Core State Standards (CCSS). That percentage certainly represents a critical mass of membership in this transformational effort. This is our chance to prove that we can thoughtfully engage in this work and really make a difference for our students and, in the long run, our nation.

## BUILDING BACKGROUND KNOWLEDGE ABOUT CCSS

For decades there have been concerted efforts to promote the development of national standards for education in the United States. For many reasons, most of them political and ideological in nature, these efforts did not gain the necessary endorsement and momentum to continue the impetus for a recommended set of common educational expectations across the states.

Beginning in the spring of 2009 all of that changed. Governors and state commissioners of education from 48 states, two territories, and the District of Columbia committed to developing a common core of state standards in English language arts and mathematics. In June 2010, after extensive study, feedback, and review, the National Governors Association and the Council of Chief State School Officers (CCSSO) released the final set of Common Core State Standards for grades K–12 in both of these critical content areas. The state-led initiative to develop these common standards grew out of concerns that the current collection of 50 different sets of state standards resulted in disparate student learning, inefficient and cumbersome allocation of resources, and a lack of rigor that does not adequately prepare our students to demonstrate readiness for college and career demands or to compete economically in a global society. The K–12 Common Core State Standards correspond to the College and Career Readiness (CCR) anchor standards, and together they define the skills and understandings necessary to adequately prepare students for life after high school.

The standards were developed in collaboration with teachers, school administrators, and content experts to provide a clear and consistent framework to prepare our children for college and the workforce. CCSS are informed by the highest, most effective models of standards from states across the nation and countries around the world, and provide teachers and parents with a common understanding of what K–12 students are expected to learn. Consistent standards will provide appropriate benchmarks for all students, regardless of where they live. They are also voluntary, meaning that states decide whether or not to adopt them; however 46 states and the District of Columbia indicate that they have accepted or will shortly accept CCSS to replace their current English language arts and mathematics state standards.

Common Core State Standards define the knowledge and skills students should have within their K–12 education experience so that they will graduate from high school able to succeed in entry-level, credit-bearing academic college courses and in career training programs. The standards

- Are aligned with college and work expectations
- Are clear, understandable, and consistent
- Include rigorous content and application of knowledge through high-order skills
- Build upon strengths and lessons of current state standards
- Are informed by other top-performing countries, so that all students are prepared to succeed in our global economy and society
- Are evidence based

The Common Core State Standards provide a consistent, clear understanding of what students are expected to learn, so teachers and parents know what they need to do to help them. The standards are designed to be robust and relevant to the real world, reflecting the knowledge and skills that our young people need for success in college and careers. With American students fully prepared for the future, our communities will be best positioned to compete successfully in the global economy. (http://www.core standards.org)

Transitioning to the new standards and the new generation assessment systems that will accompany them requires determination, vision, commitment to change, increased instructional capacity from classroom teachers and school leaders, honesty, and incredible professional dedication. It represents foundational restructuring in our K–12 educational system. For the Common Core State Standards to be effective in improving the quality of teaching and learning, states and school districts will need to rethink many current policies and practices. This process is estimated to take several years. School year 2014–2015 is the target date for both instructional implementation and administration of the new assessments created by the two consortia chosen to develop and pilot them.

The implications of the new Common Core State Standards are both exciting and overwhelming. Standards do not tell teachers how to teach and cannot by themselves ensure the quality of our nation's education system. However, they constitute an important starting point in helping schools determine the knowledge and skills that all students must be equipped with upon graduation from high school. States, districts, schools, and teachers need to begin planning now for how the new standards will impact what is currently happening in America's schools and classrooms.

## SEE THE LIGHT OR FEEL THE HEAT

Some naysayers argue that this effort is politically motivated and will give the federal government additional and unwanted power to control what is happening locally in our public school systems. Their concern and the ultimate controversy is that the long-standing tradition of retaining local control over curricular, instructional, and assessment decision making is in jeopardy. They use the unflattering term "bribery" to describe Race to the Top incentives and reveal that the potential for awarding those grants has influenced states to quickly and recklessly adopt CCSS. The worry of diminished creativity and flexibility in both the teaching and learning process is mentioned frequently.

The CCSS Initiative, in anticipation of the need for extensive communication about the initiative, has supplied factual information to assuage these fears through *A Messaging Toolkit* (see www.programs.ccsso.org/link/CCSSO/_StandardsToolkit.pdf) that addresses

- The standards themselves
- FAQs
- Myths versus facts
- A complete description of the standards development process
- Key points in English language arts and math standards
- Adopting states and their official announcements
- Statements of support
- A list of endorsing partners
- Video presentations to help inform the various publics

Of course personal and professional opinions about this topic matter a great deal. We should honor the healthy skepticism that exists. The success or failure of this reform depends largely on how we manage the commonsense implications of this dramatic change on the people who will be charged with making the system better and more responsive to our students' needs. It is time to take an honest and comprehensive look at our schools, without a defensive posture.

I am an optimist. I believe we can be informed, involved, and accountable educators, recognizing that there is challenging work to be done and requesting the required assistance for accomplishing the task without compromising our values or our sense of moral purpose. Fullan discusses the wise use of a combination of pressure and support to become comfortable with new ways of doing things. For me, that same message occurs as either focusing a light on the issues and engaging positively in the resolution of them or feeling the intense heat of failure and the dire consequences of doing nothing.

## PROGRESSIVE AND PRAGMATIC SOLUTIONS

My recommendation and in fact the focus for the rest of the book is to take what is good about the Common Core State Standards initiative and through respectful dialogue add value to its potential for improving teaching and learning in America's schools. Never before in the history of our nation have we had the option to eliminate the patchwork approach of 50 states working independently, inefficiently, and in isolation with 50 different sets of unevenly rigorous standards. We can now share collectively high expectations about what we want our K–12 students to know and be able to do in English language arts and mathematics and collaborate on the best implementation ideas to ensure that these challenging standards reach our students. We need to take advantage of this unique opportunity to work together as colleagues to

- Establish and communicate a clear set of expectations for every teacher and student
- Make it easier for students who move from school to school and state to state to experience a seamless transition, and remain confident that their consistent K–12 education leads to college or workplace success
- Boost the competitive advantage of American students, who for the first time will have the opportunity to meet the rigorous academic standards set by top-performing countries
- Create learning progressions for every grade level that are consistent and transparent to parents, students, teachers, and the general public
- Make it possible for educators to work collaboratively, coast to coast, as they adapt and enrich common standards with learning activities and best practices through professional development opportunities
- Encourage publishers and educational developers to align textbooks, digital media, and instructional materials to the rigor of Common Core State Standards

- Support the development of a unified, comprehensive, and authentic assessment system that includes both formative and summative performance tasks
- Prompt policy changes necessary to support students and teachers as they meet the challenging teaching and learning goals of the CCSS

## A CLOSER LOOK AT COMMON CORE STATE STANDARDS

Although common standards are not perfect and cannot single-handedly improve the quality of K–12 education in the United States, they set several benefits and advantages in motion. They create urgent conditions for educational innovation and reform. According to the Fordham Institute study (2010), *The State of State Standards—and the Common Core in 2010*, the Common Core State Standards are more specific and more rigorous than today's English language arts (ELA) standards (CCSSI, 2010a) in 37 states and today's math standards (CCSSI, 2010b) in 39 states. The rest of the existing standards that were compared by several agencies to CCSS were too close to call in terms of quality. So the conclusion from this data is that CCSS meets the goals of being "fewer, clearer, and higher" compared with most current state standards.

### Common Core Standards in English Language Arts

English language arts Common Core State Standards represent the best elements of exemplars collected from high-performing states and nations. Each section is divided into strands: K–5 and 6–12 ELAs have reading, writing, speaking and listening, and language strands; the 6–12 history/social studies, science, and technical subjects section focuses on content reading and writing. Each strand is introduced by a specific set of College and Career Readiness (CCR) anchor standards that is identically worded across all grades and content areas. The standards provide a clear progression of learning from kindergarten to 12th grade. They outline a vision for student literacy across all subject areas. This comprehensive framework is designed to help teachers better understand how instructional efforts at each grade level contribute to the ultimate goal of college and career readiness.

The authors of CCSS have made careful use of a vast and growing body of evidence that includes scholarly research, surveys on what skills are required of students entering college and workforce training programs, and assessment data identifying readiness for successful college and career performance. The Common Core also builds on the foundational knowledge and skills required by the National Assessment of Educational Progress (NAEP) frameworks in reading and writing.

There is clear evidence that the texts students are reading today are not of sufficient complexity to prepare them for the reading demands of the 21st century. The Common Core devotes as much attention to analyzing the difficulty of what students are reading as to how students read and comprehend the material. Most college and career reading consists of sophisticated informational text in a variety of different content areas. To address this need, the Common Core deliberately offers a significant focus on informational text in grades 6–12, and a special section designed for history/social studies and science teachers to provide knowledge in their disciplines through reading, writing, listening, and speaking.

Nonfiction writing to present an argument, or to inform or explain, is emphasized from grade six through high school after the process of writing has been mastered in elementary school. Students will also need research skills to demonstrate they can consume and produce informational media appropriately. Those standards are addressed in an interdisciplinary manner in each aspect of the curriculum rather than artificially added as a separate section.

There are three comprehensive and helpful appendices designed to assist educators and the general public in understanding the content and use of the English language arts standards for classroom instruction. These appendices provide extensive information on the research supporting the key elements of the CCSS, examples of texts to model appropriate ranges of text complexity, and annotated writing samples to illustrate proficient student performance at various grade levels.

## Common Core Standards in Mathematics

Common Core State Standards in mathematics represent a diligent effort to focus the content and provide relevance to students. The progression of learning deepens the students' abilities to comprehend and apply sophisticated mathematics in an authentic context. The Standards for Mathematical Content provide a balance of conceptual knowledge and procedural fluency offered early in a student's educational experience to allow for more concentration on and depth of understanding of the mathematical topics recognized internationally as an exit requirement of high school. The Standards for Mathematical Practice describe how students will interact with each K–12 mathematical content item regardless of the domain. They include

1. Making sense of problems and persevering in solving them

2. Reasoning abstractly and quantitatively

3. Constructing viable arguments and critiquing the reasoning of others

4. Modeling with mathematics

5. Using appropriate tools strategically

6. Attending to precision

7. Looking for and making use of structure

8. Looking for and expressing regularity in repeated reasoning

By drawing on the best models from high-performing countries, the CCSS in mathematics provide a foundation for refocusing and redesigning a coherent math curriculum that ensures the building blocks of mathematical thinking are mastered before real-world applications in algebra, geometry, probability, and statistics are introduced in middle and high school. This represents a significant difference from the current American instructional practice of "mile wide and an inch deep" coverage of numerous math topics.

As with English language arts standards, a comprehensive appendix has been developed for understanding the mathematics standards. In addition, the National Council of Teachers of Mathematics has created an excellent online teaching resource titled *Making It Happen: A Guide to Interpreting and Implementing Common Core State Standards for Mathematics* (2011). This interactive document supports K–12 educators to create a shared vision of mathematics instruction supported by CCSS.

## FROM COMMON SENSE TO COMMON PRACTICE WITH CCSS

Schools and districts will need to develop a focused and careful transition plan and a thoughtful process to implement that plan to make these standards a reality before the official roll-out deadline of 2014–2015. Leadership teams should not wait to begin the important discussions about the aspects of action planning that are within their immediate control. For instance, specific considerations for initial school-based preparation might include the following:

- Become familiar with relevant aspects of the CCSS website (http://www.corestandards.org) to gain specific information and understanding about the expectations of Common Core State Standards in English language arts and mathematics and the appendices that accompany the standards documents.

- Create a communication plan that will build advocacy and commitment to the effort by raising awareness among educators and other stakeholders using resources such as the Common Core State Standards Initiative (CCSSI) Messaging Toolkit.
- Search state departments of education websites and other online resources to collect exemplars of appropriate implementation plans and ideas that are relevant in your specific context.
- Conduct a gap and overlap cross-walk with grade-level teachers to determine the content alignment and rigor of current state standards compared with CCSS to decide what does and does not change in existing curriculum, instructional practices, and assessments
- Prepare bridge curriculum documents that map the essential content areas in English language arts and mathematics.
- Review the learning progressions that identify the grade levels or bands to discover the vertical alignment sequence of CCSS.
- Collect samples of student work to compare to CCSS and reach agreement about current levels of proficiency expectations.
- Survey teachers to assess where the critical professional learning needs are and what supports are necessary to ensure that teachers teach and students learn the knowledge and skills expected in CCSS.
- Locate or create common formative assessments and performance tasks that monitor ongoing student progress to inform daily instructional decision making.
- Integrate nonfiction writing and technology as thinking tools into every content area.
- Discuss intervention strategies with special learning service providers to ensure that all students engage with CCSS and make adequate progress.

Dozens of unanswered questions remain even after the local work begins. Some of the more pressing individual state concerns are these:

- How involved can the federal government become to support aligning, implementing, and assessing the Common Core without overstepping the tenuous boundary of education as a state responsibility?
- What processes do the National Governors Association (NGA) and CCSSO endorse for moving the implementation, sustainability, and oversight of the CCSS initiative forward in every state?

- What state-coordinated professional development opportunities will be offered?
- What budgetary impact does the CCSS initiative have on already financially strapped states?
- How will higher education work collaboratively with K–12 educators to ensure a seamless transition from high school to college or the workplace?
- Will the role of the National Assessment of Educational Progress change substantially or will the new generation of assessments replace it entirely?
- Who will determine what the state "cut scores" will be when the new assessments are administered initially?
- Will the new accountability systems reflect multiple measures of success?
- How will CCSS be governed and monitored for fidelity of implementation?
- How should special populations of learners receive the interventions necessary to support their success in meeting the more rigorous Common Core?
- How will chronically poor-performing schools and districts get assistance?

The lessons that we have learned in the past two decades with our introduction to a provisional standards-based educational system provide varied and persuasive considerations to inform our current work with CCSS. Several states have taught us that ambitious standards are not enough to raise the performance of our students. We need evidence that those rigorous standards are faithfully translated into rich instruction in our classrooms. Challenging expectations in mathematics exist in many states, but students are given choices to take alternative courses that do not address those standards to meet graduation requirements. We need to be able to ensure that students in each state are receiving the education that they require for success after high school. High-performing countries have shown us that focus on a narrower scope of content knowledge and skills provides students with a deeper understanding and ability to apply critical-thinking and problem-solving strategies to relevant and real-world learning opportunities.

So here we are at the crossroads of taking Common Core State Standards to the next level, one that will directly impact teaching and learning in our nation's classrooms. The heavy lifting is just beginning. It starts with the courageous conviction, relentless faith, and pervasive wisdom of every professional educator who potentially can bring relevance and reality to the proposed reform. That is the only way CCSS will be sustained as a viable initiative and not another failed attempt to improve our educational system.

## DO THIS NOW, DO THIS NEXT, AND DO THIS LATER

### Now . . .

Explore in depth the direct relationship of the grade level specific content mastery standards to the corresponding CCR anchor standards.

Revisit http://www.corestandards.org to review the design and organization of the documents and appendices to facilitate ease of use in instructional planning.

Explore the learning progressions for each grade level in ELA and mathematics to verify the spiraling impact of the content for vertical alignment.

### Next . . .

Reassure educators that supports and resources are being made available, including professional training and development, model curriculum, maps, pacing guides, and lesson plans. Refer to the PARCC Content Frameworks as an example of what is being created.

Acknowledge the budget constraints and concerns and the planning that will address the transitional implications of limited funding for the implementation.

Create a communication plan that will build advocacy and commitment to the effort by raising further public awareness using resources such as the CCSSI Messaging Toolkit.

### Later . . .

Conduct a needs assessment to identify the priority professional development needs that existing staff requires to deepen their knowledge of content and pedagogy aligned with the increased rigor of CCSS.

Read Mike Schmoker's book *Focus: Elevating the Essentials to Radically Improve Student Learning* (2011) as a possible book study resource to generate ideas about priority standards, content, and instructional decisions that accompany CCSS implementation considerations.

Begin creating short cycle unit assessments that provide data about student performance that is frequent and focused.

## KEY IDEAS FOR CHAPTER 3

→ We cannot afford as a society to continue to be a nation at educational risk.

→ The CCSS initiative is a state-led effort to anchor our educational system in consistent and clear educational standards for K–12 English language arts and mathematics for all students and avoid the current redundancy in effort.

→ After extensive review by several independent educational agencies, CCSS are lauded for their specificity, clarity, and rigor.

→ States have an extraordinary opportunity to intelligently pool their limited resources to co-develop curricular materials, co-build capacity in evidence-based instructional strategies, and co-create assessment systems that better reflect what students need to know and be able to do.

→ CCSS will pave the way for students to think, reflect, analyze, influence, evaluate, and communicate at high levels in both content areas.

→ Direct work with the CCSS documents and appendices will provide useful information about their design and organization.

## QUESTIONS TO CONTINUE THIS DISCUSSION

☑ From your perspective, do we remain a nation at risk of failing to prepare significant numbers of our students for college or careers after high school? Why or why not?

☑ After honest review and comparison, do your current state standards meet or exceed CCSS or do they fall short? Why or why not?

☑ How do we mobilize people to discover that in these economically challenging times, CCSS offers an opportunity to prudently share resources and expertise that support consistent expectations across our nation?

☑ What important questions remain that are essential to removing some of the obstacles to implementation in your state?

☑ Which recommended school-based planning and preparation steps are relevant and important for initiating the CCSS work in your state?

# A Relevant and Rigorous Common Core Curriculum

*This time, like all times, is a very good one,*
*if we but know what to do with it.*

—Ralph Waldo Emerson

The original Latin meaning for curriculum is "a path to run in small steps." In current educational jargon it represents on a broad scale the content taught, the resources selected, the teaching strategies employed, and the specific planned learning activities in which students engage in a classroom setting. It is often labeled the "what" of schooling and includes everything that supports student learning. A narrower definition for purposes of study in this chapter reduces the meaning to a manageable set of guidelines that address the content knowledge and skills to be learned by all students in a coherent and developmentally appropriate learning sequence or progression. Simply, a common core curriculum is an outline of what will be formally taught to all students. Chapters 5 and 6 will focus on the other aspects of curriculum that influence the development of shared frameworks in instructional strategies and next-generation assessments for use with the new common standards. For now, we will concentrate on common academic core content and skills as the intentional agenda called curriculum.

This "path that we run" will indeed require small and careful steps to arrive at the destination of a common core curriculum that is aligned with the Common Core State Standards. Advocates for beginning this journey state that all students deserve an equal opportunity to experience a high-quality education that is rich in important and comprehensive content, concepts, and skills. It is their contention that a common curriculum, one that is shared by everyone, will bond all of us together to work in concert for the benefit of our students. They believe that as a nation, we require a system whose coherence provides the new standards with defined shape and deep substance; without a common curriculum, this CCSS educational reform movement will suffer the same fate as every other improvement initiative that has failed during the last 30 years. My experience tells me these influential and prominent supporters of a common core curriculum are right.

## SOMETHING OF SUBSTANCE

Elements of an "either/or" premise linger with the challenge of establishing a rich common core of foundational knowledge and skills to align with the expectations of Common Core State Standards. Should we embrace a philosophical stance of essentialism and advocate for a content-based curriculum that honors enduring comprehensive knowledge, or do we promote a pragmatist's view of education and endorse a 21st century skills-based approach to teaching and learning? My answer is that to be thoughtfully complete, we need to consider building both educational theories into a single core curriculum framework that can support the rigor of the CCSS. We should organize teaching and learning experiences with attention to common standards and a common curriculum that utilizes traditional, intellectually ambitious liberal arts content as well as progressive, higher-order thinking skills that are emphasized in contemporary workplace contexts.

My contention is that in order to think critically about ideas and issues, to creatively and innovatively solve problems, and to communicate and collaborate about best solutions to those problems, it is essential to have something important to think about, talk about, and care about—something of substance that connects us to foundational understandings, and most important, to each other as people. As educators, we spend inordinate amounts of time seeking agreement on what is worthy of taking our valuable instructional time. I am hopeful that the current conversations about a common core curriculum will reveal our beliefs about meaningful content and direct our focus to reach consensus on the priorities that will serve our students well in the future. For me, that is a balance of rich content knowledge and the skills to fluently process those understandings and make them valuable in learning and in life.

I suggest that we combine our desire to compete with the high-performing countries we research with a willingness to take their advice and learn from them. They would teach us with indisputable evidence that learning can be useful and relevant with a content-driven comprehensive core of subject matter, that critical and creative thinking can occur in completing sophisticated project-based performance tasks, and that understanding rich content is not a distraction or diversion from an authentic education—it is the purpose of it. Higher-order thinking skills and worthwhile content knowledge are intertwined and require students to add personal perspective and reflection to powerful ideas and concepts. Educational systems such as those in Finland, Hong Kong, Singapore, and Canada have already learned this lesson: that lean guidelines for a curriculum framework can be effectively translated locally into responsive and engaging daily instruction for all students. It is our turn to reach the same logical conclusion and move forward with a common and core curriculum.

## COMMON AND CORE

Many educational reformers have acknowledged that curriculum represents the missing link in our previous 1990s work when we attempted to shift to a standard-based system that included fair and comprehensive accountability measures. We cannot afford to avoid by default having the potentially deep conversations about a common core curriculum this time around. I believe that the past controversy of principles might involve the word "common." The meaning of common need not invoke images of ordinary or even of sameness. It can legitimately refer to the metaphorical center where people meet in the middle to find common ground on which to build shared ideas and ideals.

To that end, we must position ourselves as professional educators to grapple with how this common core curriculum should evolve into deeper learning to prepare our students with the skills and knowledge necessary for future success. We need to present and advocate for the enduring concepts and content that should be taught, the shape and sequence of interdisciplinary units of study that contain those big ideas, and the critical-thinking skills to support all aspects of a comprehensive curriculum. These are not simple tasks to check off of a list or even easy conversations in which to engage because they touch our anchors, our filters, even our souls about the definition, the purpose, and our core beliefs about the value of an authentic and relevant education.

I believe the following to be some of the many benefits of defining a solid, rigorous, and coherent common core curriculum:

- Teachers can trust that if they teach a shared and agreed-upon set of knowledge and skills with fidelity, their students will be prepared for the next level of learning and will perform well on any type of assessment or accountability measure.

- Teachers can collaborate with colleagues down the hall or across state lines to share and adapt rich learning resources that will enhance the same educational expectations and opportunities.
- Parents and students can feel confident that moving to a new school or district will not disrupt the learning sequence or cause gaps or redundancy in learning.
- Teachers new to the profession can experience a meaningful preparation program and practicum that will support a teaching assignment in any state or district without the fear of being unprepared because of different grade-level expectations in content or skills.
- Texts and other learning resources can be focused and not contain hundreds of pages of nonspecific diluted and irrelevant content that is included in an attempt to match several states' content standards.
- There is more common agreement on what constitutes research-based content and appropriate learning progressions in English language arts and mathematics, so those subject areas are the logical starting points in creating common core curricula, but similar work must follow in other content areas.
- Common big ideas and essential questions provide knowledge-building content that will be enhanced and refined so students can demonstrate deeper critical thinking, problem solving, reasoning, and analytical skills.
- Curriculum guides that accent learning progressions support teachers in knowing what came before and what comes after their grade-level expectations, which assists differentiation efforts to diminish achievement gaps.
- This effort would help eliminate the "mile wide and an inch deep" content coverage phenomenon that America has embraced for several decades and experts believe is a detriment to student progress.

Some colleagues object to a common curriculum because it includes or excludes, it constrains or it frees, it prescribes or it clarifies, it is intellectual or emotional, and it takes up space or it makes room for more or less. I believe that just these dichotomies and potential contradictions alone provide legitimate reasons for why a common curriculum is crucial. It offers both structure and flexibility in our teaching and learning and allows us to use our professional judgment and creativity in ways that matter most to students. Once we think about the vital conversations regarding what a common core curriculum includes, we can push forward not to perfection, but to achievable improvement opportunities in teaching and learning.

## CONSTRUCTING THE CONVERSATION

The Common Core State Standards make it abundantly clear that they are not to be considered a curriculum. "While the Standards make references to some particular forms of content, including mythology, foundational U.S. documents, and Shakespeare, they do not, indeed cannot, enumerate all or even most of the content that students should learn. The Standards must therefore be complemented by a well-developed, content-rich curriculum consistent with the expectations laid out in this document" (Common Core State Standards Initiative, n.d.).

An impressive list of signatories endorsed a statement issued by the Albert Shanker Institute (2011) calling for common content to support the Common Core State Standards. Their recommendations include several suggestions to begin the work of creating a common core curriculum for every state, district, and school in the nation. According to these experts (Hansel, 2010–2011), we should

1. Develop one or more sets of guides that are aligned with CCSS and map out a coherent and sequenced progression of meaningful content that represents what other high-performing countries expect from all of their students at various levels

2. Ensure that teachers and content experts are involved with the development of these guides to guarantee that the context of the common core curriculum is relevant and realistic for our students and provides measureable standards of teaching quality for our teachers

3. Recognize that these guides allow for the freedom and flexibility to add important content that is expected by the local community, tailoring instruction to meet the academic needs and interests of students in their classrooms

4. Include exemplars of lesson plans and proficient student work in the guides for qualitative comparisons and leveling

5. Establish a governance agency whose members are a representative group of professional educators to oversee and evaluate the strengths and weaknesses of the common core curriculum and to supervise the revision cycle, to assess the quality and relevance of the resources and materials that support the curriculum, and to conduct research to determine the effectiveness of various curricula and instructional strategies in reaching the CCSS

6. Involve higher education to provide a seamless curricular transition from teacher preparation programs to individual classrooms

7. Increase federal resources to support the implementation of a common core curriculum and assess the value of alignment in different sequences, materials, and designs.

But these recommendations have met with significant controversy. An equally prestigious group of experts vocally countered these recommendations with their own concerns about adopting a national common core curriculum. The curriculum question is a very sensitive and debated one across our nation. There are many differing opinions about what constitutes a national curriculum and whose responsibility it is to determine and govern what students learn in their classrooms. The tradition of local control over what content and skills are presented to learners is zealously guarded in most states and has contributed to the collapse of several attempts to create nationally unified standards in the past. Common Core State Standards have reignited these feelings and have generated heated dialogue about the concept of a common set of curriculum guidelines.

Our curriculum challenge is to coordinate what the needs of our learners are with a world that demands increased rigor in what to expect from them. Complicating this task is the fact that every educator, indeed every American, has a strong opinion about what those needs and demands are. This effort represents a sea change in our beliefs about the way our educational system is structured and offers us the opportunity to make content the centerpiece of discussions about reform. Just like any other human endeavor, however, if we insist on creating a curriculum that is potentially everything to everyone, it may evolve into nothing of substance. I believe that determining what is essential can be both meaningful and mandated. We must take advantage of the permission we have been granted to provide and promote content- and skills-based learning experiences that will ensure students initially meet and ultimately exceed the expectations of the CCSS. If we articulate the learning progressions that are linked from grade to grade, we should then be able to build a defined curriculum that will allow each teacher to know what to expect from all students and to expand on what has previously been taught.

Without a balanced and aligned curriculum we risk confusion, inconsistency, loss of common knowledge, and lack of integrity of ideas. Without a common curriculum we will not benefit from the opportunities to collaborate with colleagues to build this standards-based continuity of learning. As John Dewey (1917) stated almost 100 years ago, it is "not the target but hitting the target that is the end in view" (p. 123). Oftentimes standards are viewed as targets, but we must remember that without agreement on the means to take accurate aim, we will have seriously limited our possibility of hitting a bull's eye.

## HOW THE WORLD WORKS

An elementary educator for most of my career, I am very accustomed to hearing K–5 students ask "why," seeking to discover how accurately they are fitting together all of the pieces of information that have come their way. They have an innate curiosity to explore how the world works and to make personal sense of what they learn. Secondary students ask "why" for totally different reasons. They need to see relevance and real-world authentic application and transfer to the content they are asked to learn. I propose that while we are engaging in the challenging task of defining a comprehensive curriculum that is aligned with CCSS and is both skill- and content-based, we also consider a curriculum or curricula choices that move beyond the separate subject-bound silos of information to help students see relationships, connections, and patterns and allow learning to apply coherently to their own lives.

Curriculum guidelines do not need to represent a narrow or restrictive view of learning possibilities. As with many high-performing countries such as Finland, Japan, Canada, South Korea, Australia, and New Zealand, our teachers will have the autonomy to propose an approach to curriculum and instruction designed to engage students in inquiry, promote transfer of learning, provide a conceptual framework for helping students make sense of discrete facts and skills, and uncover the big ideas of timeless content. They can choose how the essential questions will be debated and how all of these expanded understandings will transfer into new contexts and situations that personalize learning. The Common Core has established a clear view of the expectations in mathematics and English language arts. It is our responsibility as educators to translate these standards into meaningful learning experiences that represent our respect for acquiring both fluent skills and deep content knowledge, and ultimately go beyond English language and mathematics to include standards in other content areas.

## THOUGHT PARTNERS

One example of an extensive and successful curriculum reform is The New Basics Project (n.d.a), which began in 2000 by Education Queensland in Queensland, Australia, to prepare their students for 21st century learning. At that time, the endeavor dealt with necessary changes in student roles and responsibilities, recognized new economies and workforce requirements, new technologies, diverse communities, and the complexities of a new millennium. The work was very similar to what the United States is now embarking on to define CCSS. The New Basics Project targeted more rigorous learning outcomes for Australia's students. Community members, teachers, and students worked together to ensure that the richness and relevance of academic and social growth were enhanced and that there was a balance between a skills-based and a content-based approach to curriculum.

In 2004, schools throughout Queensland completed a four-year pilot of the New Basics curriculum. Those 38 schools and a selection of control schools not engaged in the trial were the subject of an extensive research project. Visit http://education.qld.gov.au/corporate/newbasics to see the complete report of the outcomes of that research.

In addition, numerous schools are currently involved with developing and implementing performance projects based on Rich Task Blueprints (The New Basics Project, n.d.b). Blueprints are innovative curriculum, assessment, and pedagogy frameworks that strive to maintain intellectual rigor and real-world connectedness while giving teachers greater flexibility and autonomy in selecting learning and performance tasks that can be used to formatively assess student progress.

I believe that even though this comprehensive research project is almost a decade old, it offers many thoughtful insights and relevant implications for our work in creating common standards and a common curriculum aligned to them. Incorporating aspects of the Rich Task Blueprints as an exemplar framework (see Exhibit 4.1) will advance the shift we need to make from command and control mandates to collaboration and connected discussions. I would encourage everyone who has an interest in curriculum design to investigate its website (http://education.qld.gov.au/corporate/newbasics/) for ideas and suggestions on how to include comprehensive content, engaging instruction, and authentic performance assessments to improve the quality of teaching and learning with our students in the United States.

Common Core's Curriculum Maps in English Language Arts is another framework that supports the new Common Core State Standards

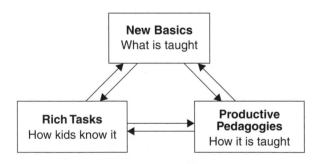

**Exhibit 4.1**     The Queensland New Basics Project

*Source:* New Zealand Ministry of Education.

for kindergarten through 12th grade. Teachers have designed practical unit maps and tools that colleagues can use to plan their instructional school year, craft their own more detailed curriculum, and create appropriate daily lesson plans. Early on during the development of the Common Core State Standards, Common Core recognized that these important and influential standards would have the potential to raise achievement for many students if they were paired with excellent curricular materials. Public school teachers created these units, and the first edition is available free of charge to anyone who would like to explore their use.

The result of this project is Common Core Curriculum Maps in ELA: a coherent sequence of thematic curriculum units, roughly six per grade level, K–12 (Gewertz, 2011). The unit maps connect the skills outlined in the CCSS in ELA with suggested works of literature and informational texts and provide activities teachers can implement immediately in their classrooms. The maps are flexible and adaptable to be responsive to local classrooms, yet they purport to thoroughly address every standard in the CCSS for ELA. Any teacher, school, or district that chooses to follow the Common Core maps is assured of adhering to the new standards. The maps are undergoing constant revision based on suggestions received from public comments and teacher reviews. The Bill and Melinda Gates Foundation funded this project.

In January 2011, the National Council of Teachers of Mathematics (NCTM) released *Making It Happen: A Guide to Interpreting and Implementing Common Core State Standards for Mathematics.* This extensive online interactive document illustrates and models the connections between the Common Core State Standards for Mathematics (CCSSM) and the NCTM's content standards. Building on the Council's decades of success in the development of standards for K–12 mathematics instruction, *Making It Happen* supports teachers, districts, and states in implementing the new Common Core mathematics standards.

*Making It Happen* is a valuable resource guide for helping educators adopt, implement, and supplement a shared position on standards, pedagogical processes, and content emphasis for mathematics instruction. Online appendices from the publication will continue to be updated as new NCTM resources become available. Many of the aims and goals of the Common Core State Standards Initiative are consistent with those of the Council's preceding work to provide all students with mathematics education of the highest quality.

Along with education policy makers, educators, and the public, national publishers of instructional materials have been watching the rollout of the Common Core State Standards with anticipation. With domestic sales of elementary and secondary textbooks and support materials accounting for $5.2 billion in 2009, according to the Association of

American Publishers, the industry has as much of a stake in the successful implementation of CCSS as their state and district customers do.

About half of the states adopt instructional materials and textbooks for their entire state, while the other half leaves the adoption of textbooks and other resources to the individual districts. Before the adoption process begins, there is much to be done to ensure a smooth transition from a current state standards-based curriculum to a common core curriculum. The plan, review, and selection procedure should include specific rubrics to assess the design standards to achieve quality control for the materials and the degree to which evidence of alignment to CCSS is provided. One of the major benefits for states adopting the Common Core is the opportunity to participate in cross-state collaboration to conduct these alignment reviews and pool resources to increase the efficiency of the critical and costly endeavor of purchasing appropriate high-quality learning materials.

Exploring the emerging use of open educational resources (OERs), which represent a network of worldwide databases that house high quality, digitized educator-developed materials and resources, is another consideration in building a resource bank to support a common core curriculum. These free materials now have more relevance and application since developers and users can focus on the common elements and expectations of the CCSS in their shared materials and ideas for implementation.

For those states and districts who elect to tackle the ambitious project of designing a local curriculum rather than relying on nationally published materials, I would recommend an in-depth study of Larry Ainsworth's book, *Rigorous Curriculum Design: How to Create Curriculum Units of Study That Align Standards, Instruction, and Assessment* (2010), as a practical guide to effectively create units of study that align with CCSS. It contains useful forms, protocols, and tools that districts have used to effectively support the step-by-step design process. Also, another helpful resource to inform curriculum design work is *Understanding by Design* by Grant Wiggins and Jay McTighe (2005). Both books are very informative and contain ideas to identify and determine desired learning goals. Many successful teams of educators choose to write their own curriculum to ensure quality and contextual relevance, and to avoid the past mistakes of implementing a textbook-driven curriculum rather than a standards-based one.

## FROM COMMON SENSE TO COMMON PRACTICE IN DEFINING A COMMON CORE CURRICULUM

Skeptics abound, and rightly so. Will we finally get it right this time around? Will 46 states and Washington, D.C., successfully work together to solve all of the inherent challenges that this movement generates? Who wouldn't question the viability of yet another even more complicated and comprehensive educational reform proposal for educators to consider? We have experimented with all varieties of ideas and innovations to improve educational outcomes without much success in the past. Does this initiative represent just another ill-conceived attempt at transforming teaching and learning in our classrooms? I believe not. Like every other veteran educator, I have participated in scores of the latest and greatest well-intentioned efforts to do more, do better, do quicker, and do easier for our students and view this common core standards, curriculum, and assessment initiative with experienced eyes. In my opinion, it is the right work for us to undertake at the right time in our educational history.

This reform effort of establishing common standards and an aligned common curriculum is urgent, elemental, and overarching, and it will have a lasting impact on the success or failure of improving student access to equity and excellence in our schools. It deserves our focused attention and should be elevated to the top of our educational agenda as an idea whose time has finally come.

## DO THIS NOW, DO THIS NEXT, AND DO THIS LATER

### Now . . .

Check out the ELA curriculum maps at http://commoncore.org/free to view exemplars that are designed as a support to the CCSS implementation efforts. The second edition of the project has a nominal fee attached to accessing the updated maps.

Begin the process of prioritizing the CCSS standards to determine which are the agreed-upon essential knowledge and skills for all students to learn and potentially reduce the number of standards to a more manageable initial set.

Begin unwrapping those priority standards using a process such as the one suggested by Larry Ainsworth to peel away the words to expose the explicit skills and content recommended in the essential standards.

### Next . . .

Design a CCSS grade-level unit of study that supports a big idea using a project-based learning approach and performance tasks to assess student progress.

Create curriculum maps that indicate a logical pace and progression that can potentially be aligned with the priority standards that have been selected from CCSS.

Enhance the opportunities for professional learning communities of grade-level and vertical teams to review the current implications for CCSS implementation.

## Later . . .

Collaboratively investigate your current curriculum to define whether it represents the level of depth and focus that is recommended by many educational advocates.

Begin incorporating the Mathematical Practices endorsed in CCSSM with an existing mathematics program or curriculum.

Explore how to incorporate reading, writing, and discussion into all content areas.

## KEY IDEAS FOR CHAPTER 4

→ A curriculum is a very complex educational concept that broadly represents anything which supports student learning, but it is typically associated with the progression of common knowledge and skills that are enduring and essential for success in life.

→ Curriculum decision making and design involves value judgments and beliefs about the purpose of schooling.

→ A core curriculum is a new phenomenon in the United States, but high-performing nations have experience in adopting common and comprehensive content goals and using them to guide the teaching and learning experiences in their classrooms.

→ The debate of a skills-based curriculum versus a content-based one needs to be resolved with the realization and acceptance that both are critical elements in a comprehensive education.

→ The benefits of a common core curriculum establish a platform for sharing curriculum design ideas, expertise, and the resources of time and funding across state lines.

→ Several thought partners have already engaged in creating support materials and resources that will inform and expedite the work of establishing a common core curriculum.

## QUESTIONS TO CONTINUE THIS DISCUSSION

- ☑ How do the interpretation and many definitions of the word *curriculum* support or interfere with the work of reaching common agreements and common ground about what will be taught to our students?
- ☑ How would a debate about the importance and relationship between a content-based and a skills-based curriculum be resolved in your educational context?
- ☑ How do we reach consensus about the "what" that we expect all highly educated American students to have learned at the end of their public K–12 educational experience?
- ☑ What specific knowledge and skills defines the day-to-day work of teaching and learning in our classrooms?
- ☑ How does the difficult and challenging task of simplifying what we teach to rich and coherent content begin?
- ☑ How is shared meaning reached about the myriad of questions that involve curriculum; what are the big ideas, essential questions, cogent vocabulary, and appropriate resources to identify a common body of knowledge?

# Inviting Students to Learn

5

*I hear, and I forget;*
*I see, and I remember;*
*I do, and I understand.*

—Confucius

I was initially perplexed by the struggle I was experiencing drafting and revising this essential chapter about instruction. I naively thought this would be the easiest of the nine chapters for me to write because of my background with this topic. I thought I knew instruction inside and out. I can recognize and appreciate what actually happens in dynamic classrooms between talented teachers and motivated students who make learning come alive for everyone because of supervising scores of them. I have observed instructional magic thousands of times over the course of my career in education, and I made a little of my own, by the way. I have taught both preservice and master's-level teachers about considerations in professional practice. So when I confronted the challenge of putting my ideas on paper about how to think about effective teaching, I was amazed by the many back-up and start-over moments I encountered.

The view that teaching is simple, straightforward, and routine is both uninformed and inaccurate. That understanding might provide one very basic explanation for why my test to rationalize and reduce the work of teaching to finite steps is proving to be impossible. Linda Darling-Hammond (1997) thoughtfully describes teaching as complex and sophisticated work, characterized by "simultaneity, multidimensionality, and unpredictability" (p. 69). Teaching decisions have competing goals, multiple tasks, and trade-offs involving obstacles and opportunities that are negotiated at a breakneck pace. Every day teachers are required to juggle the need to create a safe and secure environment for learning with the pressure of reaching higher academic achievement targets; to balance the needs of the individual students with that of the group; and to respond to the diverse needs and interests of all learners whose readiness to learn lies in varying places of development.

There is no recipe or formula to follow for implementing quality instruction. The fundamental premise for an effective classroom is simple—teachers teach and learners learn—but anyone who knows teaching intimately understands that engaging students by meeting them where they are and taking them forward is a very complicated endeavor. The interactive process that teachers skillfully navigate when they match appropriate learning experiences to students with unique learning needs is central to understanding how good instruction affects achievement.

The authors of the Common Core State Standards demonstrate a hearty respect for the intricacies of instruction by explicitly stating that "teachers are thus free to provide students with whatever tools and knowledge their professional judgment and experience identify as most helpful for meeting the goals set out in the standards. The standards define what all students are expected to know and be able to do but not how teachers should teach" (Common Core State Standards Initiative, n.d.). Giving this flexibility and freedom is a gift of esteem to most teachers, but it is a burden to others who are less confident and experienced in making the high-yield instructional decisions that will most likely enhance student achievement.

Teaching has been a traditionally private profession. Until just recently, with the advent of professional learning communities and other means to foster ways of discussing and sharing our practice, we have become more public, but typically we still do our work in isolation with limited opportunities to collaboratively define or articulate what the craft knowledge of teaching really is. No knowledge base will ever provide all of the information necessary to guarantee a teacher's success, and the Common Core initiative acknowledges that fact. However, unlike other countries, we in the United States have resisted creating a shared and verified professional language that describes teaching knowledge and skill. This lack of a common language makes it difficult to advance our discussion of what teaching strategies work best for students. John Hattie, Robert Marzano, and others have helped open classroom doors by systematically analyzing and synthesizing what is happening behind them to improve learning and to discover some common best practices that should be replicated in classrooms everywhere.

The remainder of this chapter provides some "probability-based guidance," as W. James Popham (2008) mentions, which represents evidence-based instructional considerations that positively influence student learning. These understandings form the basis of observed adult behaviors and practitioner knowledge that can be accumulated, shared, assessed, and available for the benefit of students across the nation. It is exciting to finally have a deliberate reason and opportunity to reflect on our own teaching practice and go public with ideas that are powerful and contribute to dramatically increased student learning.

## THE POWER OF DEEPLY UNDERSTANDING INSTRUCTION

It has taken me years of study and reflection to reach three very logical and seemingly uncomplicated conclusions about effective instruction: It involves knowing the learner intimately; it involves knowing the content thoroughly; and finally, it involves knowing instructional approaches fluently that artfully and meaningfully convey that content. The illustration below (the Teaching Triangle) indicates how simplistic these understandings should be, but realistically these instructional decisions are very intricate and represent the elegance of teaching.

Knowing your learners is at the top of this triangle; without current and accurate knowledge of the students' learning strengths and challenges and the students' interests and attitudes toward the content, you could spend inordinate amounts of time planning and implementing an elaborate lesson and the wrong learners show up. Students who do not have the prerequisite knowledge or skills to be successful with the lesson, or students who have already mastered the content, do not

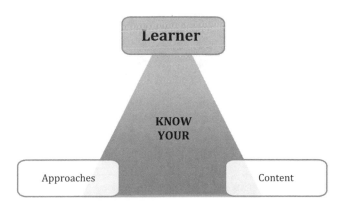

benefit from even the most engaging learning experience that is not on target. Knowing your learners well implies that you collect data about their current level of performance and plan appropriate instruction accordingly.

The Leadership and Learning Center has created a step-by-step framework that helps identify teaching strategies that become measureable indicators of student learning (see Exhibit 5.1). The Data Teams process offers a structured cycle of collaborative data review that asks the right questions to help discover the right answers about what to teach, how to teach it, how to meet individual student needs, and how to confidently implement instructional strategies that work for both teachers and students. I would encourage colleagues to investigate this dynamic process of examining student strengths and needs to make informed instructional decisions that ensure better learning for all students in the book *Leaders Make It Happen! An Administrator's Guide to Data Teams,* by Brian McNulty and Laura Besser (2011). As illustrated in this resource, when this process is implemented deliberately and consistently, Data Teams has proven to be a practical and effective strategy to improve teaching and learning in schools.

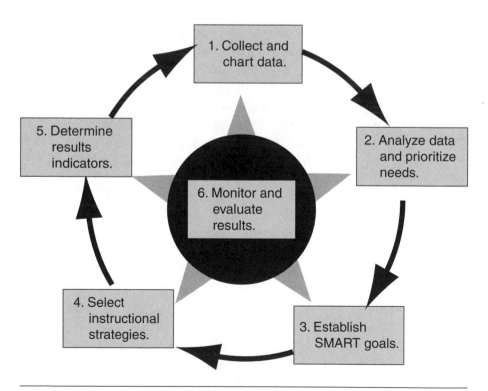

**Exhibit 5.1**  The Data Teams Process
*Source:* Rose et al. (2010).

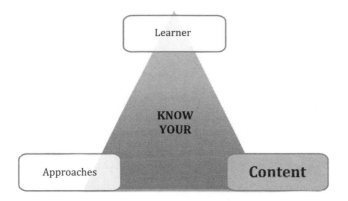

The second point on the triangle (above) identifies how important a teacher's thorough knowledge of the content is to learning success. We spent a lengthy time in Chapter 4 discussing what role curriculum plays in this educational reform, so I will not belabor it here. Common Core State Standards will guide and direct our efforts to determine what content and skills are necessary to meet the rigorous national standards, but we cannot be sideline participants in this conversation. Who better to know what grade-level content best supports the ELA and mathematics standards than teachers in classrooms? Who better to determine the scope and sequence of the learning progressions than the professionals who differentiate instruction daily to meet the needs of all learners? It is imperative that we lend our expertise and energy to defining what content adds richness and relevance to the learning experience at each level.

The Partnership for the Assessment of Readiness for College and Careers (PARCC) has created the PARCC Model Content Frameworks in English Language Arts/Literacy and Mathematics. These frameworks have been developed through a collaborative state-led process between state curriculum experts and members of the Common Core State Standards writing teams and are an excellent content resource for CCSS implementation considerations. The model content frameworks are designed to serve several purposes. They help identify the big ideas in the Common Core State Standards for each grade level, they help determine the focus for the various PARCC assessment components, and they will support the future development of the PARCC assessment blueprints.

And now, let's move on to the third and final point on the Teaching Triangle (see page 64): instructional approaches that support quality learning. Through experience and experimenting, all educators discover certain instructional strategies that work well for them. They take pride in

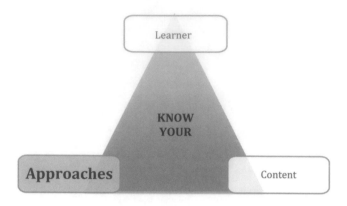

expanding their teaching toolkit to include engaging methods of behavior and response that establish powerful conditions for learning that are meaningful for their students. We have had some significant advice in discovering certain research-based teaching strategies that have proven to enhance learning. The most widely accepted resource on this topic is *Classroom Instruction That Works: Research-Based Strategies for Increasing Student Achievement* (2001), written by Robert Marzano, Debra Pickering, and Jane Pollock. The nine strategies they identify have formed the basis of conversations about instruction and offer a starting point for our discussion. The nine strategies are the following:

- Identifying similarities and differences
- Summarizing and taking notes
- Reinforcing effort and providing recognition
- Homework and practice
- Nonlinguistic representations such as graphic organizers and physical models
- Cooperative learning
- Setting objectives and providing feedback
- Generating/testing hypotheses
- Questions, cues, and advance organizers

Marzano (2009) wisely cautions us, however, in a *Phi Delta Kappan* article that we must shift to a comprehensive framework or language of instruction that is the source of professional conversations and the subject of increasing student achievement. We must go beyond simplistic checklists of instructional strategies if we are to improve teaching and learning. These words of wisdom are valuable insights into the fact that there is no magic instructional strategy that works equally well in all situations with all students. A prudent teacher must select from a wide variety of research-based strategies and approaches that focus on increasing student achievement when they are used effectively during classroom instruction.

One of the most utilitarian and authentic strategies is teaching students how to write well. The new emphasis and expectation in the Common Core demands that this skill be integrated into every discipline so that the writing–thinking–learning connection will be strengthened.

## THE POWER OF DEEPLY IMPLEMENTING NONFICTION WRITING

Language is central to all learning. As human beings, our sophisticated use of symbols and labels allows us to communicate ideas, beliefs, and emotions with each other, and without a significant proficiency with language we cannot succeed in school or in life. The authors of CCSS thoughtfully and comprehensively emphasize the importance of literacy to be college and career ready at the end of the high school experience. They also boldly suggest that literacy instruction is too immense for just the trained language arts teachers to handle and that literacy standards for grade 6 and above are predicated on teachers of ELA, history/social studies, science, and technical subjects using their content area expertise to help students meet the particular challenges of reading, writing, speaking, listening, and language in their respective fields.

The Common Core State Standards for English Language Arts and Literacy in History/Social Studies, Science, and Technical Subjects (Common Core State Standards Initiative, 2010a) reinforce the importance of becoming a literate citizen, one who reads with understanding, writes with clarity, and speaks, listens, and uses language effectively. Most notably in these standards as compared with many current state standards is the increased emphasis on the ability of students to compose argumentative or persuasive essays proficiently. "The ability to write logical arguments based on substantive claims, sound reasoning, and relevant evidence is a cornerstone of the writing standards, with opinion writing a basic form of writing, extending down into the earliest grades. Research, both short focused projects, such as those commonly required in the workplace, and longer-term in-depth research is emphasized throughout the standards, but most prominently in the writing strand since a written analysis and presentation of findings is so often critical. Annotated samples of student writing accompany the standards and help establish adequate performance levels in writing arguments, informational and explanatory texts, and narratives in the various grades."

Douglas Reeves has been an assertive and staunch advocate for frequent, interdisciplinary nonfiction writing instruction as a viable link to enhanced critical thinking and higher student achievement in all content areas. He states in *Reason to Write* (2002):

- Writing can activate background knowledge.
- Writing can increase engagement, especially when used in conjunction with talking and sharing activities.
- Students can feel more in control of their learning when using writing regularly.
- Writing, more than any other subject, can lead to personal breakthroughs in learning.
- Writing is a highly complex act that demands the analysis and synthesis of many levels of thinking.
- Writing develops initiative. In reading, everything is provided. In writing, the learner must supply everything.
- Writing develops courage. At no point is the learner more vulnerable than in writing.
- Writing can contribute to reading from the first day of school.
- Writing contributes strongly to reading comprehension, as children grow older.
- The ability to revise writing for greater power and economy is one of the higher forms of reading.
- Writing contributes to a sense of connection and personal efficacy by participation in society.
- Writing, particularly with evaluation, editing, revision, and rewriting, will improve the ability of a student to communicate and succeed on state and local writing assessments.

A powerful listing, wouldn't you agree? Mike Schmoker (2006) aligns his endorsement with Dr. Reeves by stating how important writing is to cultivating students' critical-thinking ability and preparing them for the rigors of college, civic life, and careers. "Generous amounts of close, purposeful reading, rereading, writing, and talking are the essence of authentic literacy. These simple activities are the foundation for a trained, powerful mind and a promising future" (p. 53). Finally, in K–12 education, we are beginning to pay attention to the evidence-based imperative that writing is thinking and clarity in both is a feature of deep understanding. The intellectual struggle in which students engage when making new content their own involves wrestling with information to find the individual fit that makes sense to them, and the ability to communicate those personal connections to peers and teachers through writing is crucial.

"If you cannot write well, you cannot think well, and if you cannot think well, others will do your thinking for you." George Orwell had that right, and his message to us as educators is that all of our students deserve the competence and confidence to write well so that they can participate in society in a meaningful and informed way. Equal access to the skills of expository writing to support claims with evidence; to argue for a particular position; and to examine and convey ideas, concepts, and information are the abilities necessary to master the language of the educated and will open the pathways to intellectual, economic, and political power. Meeting and exceeding the CCSS in English language arts is the best way to ensure that our students are prepared to successfully have control over the logic and quality of their thoughts and ideas. We must give them nothing less.

## THE POWER OF DEEPLY UTILIZING DIMENSIONS OF LEARNING

I am all for resurrecting relevant and authentic ideas from the past. It is a bit like re-wearing the classic little black dress or the navy-blue pinstriped suit that has been a mainstay in your wardrobe for years. It is still in style, still fits, and still gets compliments. For me, *A Different Kind of Classroom: Teaching With Dimensions of Learning* is the "little black dress" for educators. Written in 1992 by Robert Marzano, its usefulness as an instructional model with implementation implications for the Common Core is as applicable now as it was two decades ago.

Dimensions of Learning (McREL, n.d.) is a comprehensive framework to assist teachers in planning rich learning experiences for their students. It is based on extensive research about learning and how the mind works. It is designed to improve students' learning using five critical aspects of the learning process, or dimensions of learning. They are

- Attitudes and Perceptions About Learning
- Acquisition and Integration of Knowledge
- Extension and Refinement of Knowledge
- Meaningful Use of Knowledge
- Productive Habits of the Mind

### Dimension 1: Attitudes and Perceptions About Learning

Attitudes and perceptions dramatically affect students' ability to learn effectively. For example, if students view the classroom as an unsafe place to take risks in learning, they will likely learn little there. Similarly, if students have negative attitudes about instructional tasks, they will inevitably put little effort into those experiences. A key consideration in effective instruction is helping students to establish positive attitudes and perceptions about the classroom learning environment and about learning itself.

## Dimension 2: Acquisition and Integration of Knowledge

Helping students acquire and integrate new knowledge is another critical element of the learning process. When students are learning new information, they must be shown how to relate that new knowledge to what they already know, organize that information, and then make it part of their long-term memory. When students are acquiring new skills and processes, they must learn a model or set of steps, and then shape the skill or process to make it personally efficient and effective for them, and, finally, internalize or practice the skill or process so they can perform it automatically, accurately, and fluently.

## Dimension 3: Extension and Refinement of Knowledge

Learning does not stop with acquiring and integrating knowledge. Learners develop in-depth understanding through the process of extending and refining their knowledge, that is, by making new distinctions, clearing up misconceptions, and reaching conclusions. They rigorously analyze what they have learned by applying reasoning processes that will help them extend and refine the information. Some of the common reasoning processes used by learners to extend and refine their knowledge are the following:

- Comparing
- Classifying
- Abstracting
- Inductive reasoning
- Deductive reasoning
- Constructing support
- Analyzing errors
- Analyzing perspectives

## Dimension 4: Meaningful Use of Knowledge

The most effective learning occurs when we use knowledge to perform meaningful tasks. For example, we might initially learn about snowboards by talking to a friend or reading a magazine article about them. We really learn about them, however, when we are trying to decide what kind of snowboard to purchase. Making sure that students have the opportunity to use knowledge meaningfully is one of the most important parts of planning a unit of instruction. In the Dimensions of Learning model, there are six reasoning processes around which tasks can be constructed to encourage the meaningful use of knowledge:

- Decision making
- Problem solving
- Invention
- Investigation
- Experimental inquiry
- Systems analysis

## Dimension 5: Productive Habits of the Mind

The most effective learners have developed powerful habits of mind that enable them to think critically, think creatively, and regulate their behavior. These mental habits are listed below:

### Critical Thinking

- Be accurate and seek accuracy
- Be clear and seek clarity
- Maintain an open mind
- Restrain impulsivity
- Take a position when the situation warrants it
- Respond appropriately to others' feelings and level of knowledge

### Creative Thinking

- Persevere
- Push the limits of your knowledge and abilities
- Generate, trust, and maintain your own standards of evaluation
- Generate new ways of viewing a situation that are outside the boundaries of standard conventions

### Self-Regulated Thinking

- Monitor your own thinking
- Plan appropriately
- Identify and use necessary resources
- Respond appropriately to feedback
- Evaluate the effectiveness of your actions

As indicated in Exhibit 5.2, the first and fifth dimensions influence all learning and are important contributors to students' sense of efficacy. Before students can effectively attend to dimensions 2, 3, and 4, they must form positive attitudes and perceptions about learning and develop productive habits of mind. The Common Core State Standards in English

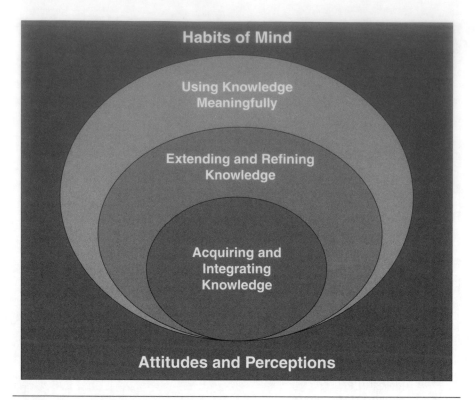

**Exhibit 5.2**    Dimensions of Learning

McREL. (n.d.). What is Dimensions of Learning and How is it Used? Retrieved from
http://www.mcrel.org/dimensions/whathow.asp
Copyright McREL. Used by permission of McREL.

language arts and mathematics also indicate habits of mind that support
deep learning and meet the rigor of the standards.

---

In developing knowledge and skills in English language arts,
learners

Demonstrate independence

Build strong content knowledge

Respond to the varying demands of audience, task, purpose,
and discipline

Comprehend as well as critique

Value evidence

Use technology and digital media strategically and capably

Come to understand other perspectives and cultures

*(Common Core State Standards Initiative, 2010a)*

In developing knowledge and skills in mathematics, learners

Make sense of problems and persevere in solving them

Reason abstractly and quantitatively

Construct viable arguments and critique the reasoning of others

Model with mathematics

Use appropriate tools strategically

Attend to precision

Look for and make use of structure

Look for and express regularity in repeated reasoning

*(Common Core State Standards Initiative, 2010b)*

I feel it is appropriate to include the Dimensions of Learning model as a valuable representation for the learning process and a vital support to the work of preparing for the implementation of the CCSS. The challenge of translating this educational reform into practice is huge; unless we break it down into manageable chunks, it will overwhelm us and obstruct our ability to move forward. What is encouraging and edifying is that elements of good instruction are an essential part of this initiative and will focus our efforts on the right work of educating all students to their maximum potential.

## THE POWER OF DIFFERENTIATION

The academic diversity of students in American schools has never been greater. Teachers are required to differentiate the expectations for content, process, and work products based on their knowledge of an individual student's readiness, background and experience with language and abilities, or learning challenges. Carol Ann Tomlinson offers legitimate considerations for how to accomplish this instructional responsibility in her seminal work, *The Differentiated Classroom: Responding to the Needs of All Learners* (1999).

Tomlinson's commonsense approach to differentiation confirms my beliefs that when you "take the lid off learning" for all students and raise academic and behavioral expectations, the results are surprising. Dr. Tomlinson identifies this as creating "respectful tasks" and "teaching up" and indicates that all students deserve the good stuff—the rich and engaging knowledge and skills that are essential for success. With the right amount of scaffolding of time and opportunity, students can make sense of their world; see how all of the pieces fit together; and most important, understand how this new learning connects with their own lives.

Many authors have attempted to flatten the understanding of instruction, but it refuses to be minimized. We need to take deliberate time to discuss our effective instructional practices and extend our repertoire of teaching strategies that work well for our students and for us. These conversations can be some of the most meaningful and memorable of any professional dialogues that occur in schools with teams of colleagues.

## FROM COMMON SENSE TO COMMON PRACTICE IN INSTRUCTION

We are always challenged as educators to translate what we know about teaching and learning into actions that prove what we believe is possible with our students. We are frequently accused of being indifferent to research and ignoring what is germane to improved learning outcomes for our students. In defense of some of this reluctance to accept all of these sometimes conflicting theories is the fact that teachers are requested to bring clarity to the vague and sometimes hazy sense of how to define what great instruction is. How do we deliberately create learning experiences that engage learners and provide the necessary knowledge and skills to allow them to progress to the next level of understanding? How do we apply the language of instruction and craft knowledge to our work? How do we create climates for learning that promote risk taking and acknowledge how vulnerable learners are? These are deep and complicated questions and need deeper and more consistently shared answers.

Active learning entices, motivates, and enchants both students and adults, but the bottom line is that we can provide the opportunity, the environment, and the encouragement, but the learning belongs ultimately to the learner. My experience with teaching and learning indicates that certain conditions must be present to optimize it. What I know to be true is that students need to consistently

- Feel connected
- Feel cared about
- Feel significant with others
- Feel competent with others
- Feel listened to
- Know they will be missed if absent
- Know they can contribute with value if present
- Feel accepted and respected for who they are
- Feel supported and challenged

Instruction must emphasize personal meaning and understanding. It begins with student interests and their essential questions about how the world works and ends with learning experiences that are organized around real-life problems and projects. Exploration is active and interactive, individual and social. Indicators of thinking and motivation through students' actual demonstrations of what they know and can do assess success. These are easy words but difficult behaviors.

Dennis Littky (2004) has helped me expand my list of the real and legitimate goals of education. To do this, I began just as CCSS encourages us to imagine our students as productive adults. What would they need to enjoy future success in college, careers, and life? Here is partial list, and I think it behooves each of us to create our own list and revisit it frequently to guide and refocus our work with students. I believe this process will help us clarify what we do and lift some of that haze that surrounds our profession. We need to support students to become

- Lifelong learners
- Passionate about understanding how the world works
- Ready to take risks in learning and exploring new ideas
- Creative problem solvers and critical thinkers
- Tolerant of different ideas and perceptions
- Independent and interdependent workers
- Caring and compassionate about people and our planet
- Persistent and able to persevere on difficult tasks
- Moral, respectful, and courageous citizens
- Literate and numerate
- Joyful people who enjoy life and work

Well, this chapter on instruction is finally finished and in retrospect I have determined why writing it was met with such fits and starts, stutters and stammers. Without answering the generative question about *why* the knowledge of instruction is so important, educators are in jeopardy of missing the fundamental point of our mission. We have the humbling responsibility of enhancing and enriching the learning and the lives of our students. There are some undeniable evidence-based strategies that help us accomplish this awe-inspiring task. Discussions about how to implement the Common Core State Standards give us the opportunity to reach some common agreements and seek some common language and common ground about the vital work we do.

## DO THIS NOW, DO THIS NEXT, AND DO THIS LATER

### Now . . .

Begin a focused study of the appendices included in both the English language arts and mathematics standards to explore the depth of the promise of "fewer, clearer, and more rigorous standards."

Begin aligning current instructional resources to CCSS.

Begin designing engaging learning experiences for students that align with one CCSS big idea and essential question.

### Next . . .

Begin to scrutinize the PARCC Content frameworks that contain summaries of CCSS and what students need to know and be able to do with them at the end of each year.

Create reading and writing progressions that indicate the number of short texts and full-length books that meet the requirements of CCSS as well as the percentage of time students need to write about analytical and narrative materials.

Begin increasing argumentative writing across all areas of the curriculum and at every level.

### Later . . .

Refer to the PTA's Guides for Student Success (www.pta.org/PublicPolicy) as a helpful resource for parents to engage with CCSS.

Begin the challenging discussion about how to support all learners through differentiation of instruction.

Commit to developing quarterly units of study that incorporate big ideas, essential questions, and academic vocabulary from CCSS.

## KEY IDEAS FOR CHAPTER 5

→ Teaching is complex and sophisticated work and requires flexibility in making the myriad of instructional decisions that are necessary to manage an effective classroom.

→ The authors of the CCSS realize that there is no recipe for instruction and trust teachers to have the ability to be responsive to their students' unique learning needs.

→ We need to engage in public and collaborative conversations to create a professional language that comprehensively defines our work with students.

→ Good teaching must consider knowing your learners, knowing your content, and knowing instructional strategies that support learning that content.

→ Among the abstract beliefs that individual educators hold about teaching and learning are very concrete, evidence-based strategies that work effectively with learners.

→ Nonfiction writing is essential to clarify thinking.

→ Dimensions of Learning help to organize educators' thoughts about the components of instruction that contribute to enhanced learning.

## QUESTIONS TO CONTINUE THIS DISCUSSION

☑ How do the specific strategies mentioned in this chapter support learning for the diverse learners we see in every classroom?

☑ How do we develop a common language of instruction so we can converse with each other?

☑ What are your personal and professional goals for education?

☑ How do opportunities to share beliefs and practices about effective instruction build a learning community?

☑ How do we begin to build background knowledge about CCSS that includes the essential what, why, how, and when questions that will directly impact the level of student engagement with CCSS?

# Powerful Professional Learning for Adults

*The biggest effect on student learning occurs when teachers become learners of their own teaching, and when students become their own teachers.*

—John Hattie

It is difficult for us as educators to admit we struggle to define something as basic as effective professional development that improves our teaching practices and results in increased student learning. We have all personally experienced different models or types of staff training, probably been coached and mentored at some time in our careers, and most likely participated in one or more professional learning communities designed to support our work with students. The findings from research do little to help us describe the elusiveness of what separates truly engaging, meaningful, and sustainable professional learning experiences from irrelevant and poorly executed ones. Thomas Guskey (2000, p. ix) states: "Over the years, a lot of good things have been done in the name of professional development. So have a lot of rotten things. What professional developers have not done is provide evidence to document the difference between the good and the rotten." He suggests five sequenced levels to evaluate professional development, and his insight will go far in influencing how we handle the comprehensive professional learning needs that will be a necessary catalyst for implementing the Common Core State Standards reforms.

Guskey also notes that worthwhile and well-designed professional development is intentional and ultimately focused on improved student learning, is ongoing and embedded in our daily practice, is supported through follow-up and feedback, and is collaborative and collegial. It must be viewed as integral to teaching well and directly linked to solving

**Exhibit 6.1**  Five Levels of Professional Development Evaluation

| Evaluation Level | What Questions Are Addressed? | How Will Information Be Gathered? | What Is Measured or Assessed? | How Will Information Be Used? |
|---|---|---|---|---|
| 1. Participants' Reactions | Did they like it? Was their time well spent? Did the material make sense? Will it be useful? Was the leader knowledgeable and helpful? Were the refreshments fresh and tasty? Was the room the right temperature? Were the chairs comfortable? | Questionnaires administered at the end of the session | Initial satisfaction with the experience | To improve program design and delivery |
| 2. Participants' Learning | Did participants acquire the intended knowledge and skills? | Paper-and-pencil instruments Simulations Demonstrations Participant reflections (oral and/or written) Participant portfolios | New knowledge and skills of participants | To improve program content, format, and organization |
| 3. Organization Support and Change | What was the impact on the organization? Did it affect organizational climate and procedures? Was implementation advocated, facilitated, and supported? Was the support public and overt? Were problems addressed quickly and efficiently? | District and school records Minutes from follow-up meetings Questionnaires Structured interviews with participants and district or school administrators Participant portfolios | The organization's advocacy, support, accommodation, facilitation, and recognition | To document and improve organizational support To inform future change efforts |

**Exhibit 6.1** (Continued)

| Evaluation Level | What Questions Are Addressed? | How Will Information Be Gathered? | What Is Measured or Assessed? | How Will Information Be Used? |
|---|---|---|---|---|
| | Were sufficient resources made available? Were successes recognized and shared? | | | |
| 4. Participants' Use of New Knowledge and Skills | Did participants effectively apply the new knowledge and skills? | Questionnaires Structured interviews with participants and their supervisors Participant reflections (oral and/or written) Participant portfolios Direct observations Video or audio tapes | Degree and quality of implementation | To document and improve the implementation of program content |
| 5. Student Learning Outcomes | What was the impact on students? Did it affect student performance or achievement? Did it influence students' physical or emotional well-being? Are students more confident as learners? Is student attendance improving? Are dropouts decreasing? | Student records School records Questionnaires Structured interviews with students, parents, teachers, and/ or administrators Participant portfolios | Student learning outcomes: <br> • Cognitive (Performance & Achievement) <br> • Affective (Attitudes & Dispositions) <br> • Psychomotor (Skills & Behaviors) | To focus and improve all aspects of program design, implementation, and follow-up To demonstrate the overall impact of professional development |

Guskey, T. R. (2000). *Evaluating Professional Development.* Thousand Oaks, CA: Corwin Press.

authentic problems of practice that are defined by the gaps between what actually occurs in our nation's classrooms and what we desire and hope for our students.

If we are to get this CCSS reform initiative right this time around and have teachers successfully teach all students to substantially higher levels of rigor, then virtually everyone who is responsible for boosting student learning outcomes must also be learning virtually all of the time as well. Professional development can no longer be uneven, disconnected, arbitrary, or limited. It requires a systematic approach that supports, develops, and mobilizes the talent that already exists in our classrooms. How we orchestrate this effort and provide the evidence that student learning does increase as a result of enhanced adult instructional skillfulness and content understanding will determine a new credibility and a new commitment to quality professional development experiences. How we demystify the issue so that professional learning can receive a fresh start and a fair shake depends on our ability to sensitively acknowledge that most learning occurs through experimentation and error in actual practice and typically cannot be delivered in one-shot seminars. Learning is not a linear or a solo process and requires building a culture of trust that nurtures individual and group reflection, responsibility, and respect.

I have observed the rolled eyes and the accompanying cynicism that indicate the lukewarm reception and reaction that certain professional learning opportunities evoke. I am also well aware of how entrenched a teaching culture can become without deliberate attention to creating robust conversations about the quality of student work, curriculum, assessment, lesson and unit design, data use, and building competence and confidence to become more successful at the work of teaching in general. I have witnessed and participated in poorly conceived and deeply flawed exercises that were loosely labeled as staff development training. As a result, I know we have extensive promotional work to do to convince both veteran and novice educators that we can create a flexible and fluent framework that contributes to everyone's capacity to learn new content and processes, and ultimately develop the new expertise necessary to thoughtfully and thoroughly implement Common Core State Standards.

Professional development should be a vital part of the overall strategy for school improvement and not just a catalogue of isolated and discrete activities that have no relationship to each other or any bearing on the quality of student learning. Formally, professional development is described by many as a set of knowledge- and skill-building events that increase the capacity of teachers and administrators to respond to external demands and to engage in the improvement of practices and performance. A central part of the practice of improvement should be to make the connection between instruction and student learning more obvious, direct, and clear. "The present generation of students deserves the best practice we can give them and their learning should not be mortgaged against the probability that something good will happen for future generations. Improvement should be focused directly on the classroom experience of today's students." This was Richard Elmore's belief in 2002, but it perhaps has more relevance and reality today in our discussions about the vast professional development implications for implementing the CCSS initiative.

## ADULT LEARNING THEORY

Adult learners are by nature autonomous and self-directed. They need to have the creative freedom and flexibility to guide their own learning and direct themselves to personal new understandings and skills. Specifically, they must have control over what topics to explore and be encouraged to work on authentic projects that reflect their personal and professional interests and strengths. Adults desire to be the origin of their own learning and will resist learning activities they believe are a criticism of their competence. Thus, effective professional development needs to give participants some choice over the what, who, how, why, when, and where of their learning.

Adult learners are relevancy and reality oriented. They must see a legitimate reason and immediate value for expending time and energy to learn something that potentially will enhance their performance. Learning has to be directly applicable and connected to their daily work to be useful. Adults will commit to professional learning when the goals and objectives are clearly defined and considered genuinely realistic, relevant, and related to their personal story and their current professional needs.

Adult learners are socially motivated. They have the need to feel significant and competent with their colleagues, to have ample opportunities to lead and to follow. Professional development must be structured to provide support from peers and to reduce the fear of public embarrassment and judgment when learning something new. Adults need to receive specific, timely, accurate, and constructive feedback on how they are doing and the obvious positive differences they are making in student achievement as a result of their investment in new learning. Opportunities must be built into professional development activities that support extensive and coached practice and follow-up. Adults need to participate in professional dialogue groups during the learning process to deepen their understanding and support each other's growth.

Adult learners are practical and time-bound. They desire to see immediate and focused alignment and thoughtful coherence built into the external expectations that comply with the professional learning demands of the system. They need transparent evidence that the new learning will benefit students and that they will be respected at wherever their learning entrance is. Adults want to observe the benchmarked behaviors modeled and demonstrated by experts so that they can receive the scaffolded support necessary to feel competent and confident in the new practice or skill.

Adult learners are sophisticated with a wide range of previous experiences, knowledge, self-direction, interests, and competencies. This diversity must be acknowledged and accommodated in professional development planning. These adults should be respected for their level of expertise and allowed to voice their opinions freely to enhance the richness of the professional learning opportunity for everyone by sharing, reflecting, and generalizing about the topic (White, 2009).

## IMPLICATIONS FOR PROFESSIONAL DEVELOPMENT

Since the demands of the Common Core State Standards are so tightly woven into a comprehensive framework for increased professional learning, educators who are truly invested in the success of this initiative need to consider how to plan, organize, and implement quality and differentiated support for classroom teachers, school and district leaders, and policy makers. To do this intelligently, we must consider the common ground in content and process expertise that already exists in each unique state and district context. No one, certainly me included, can presume to externally prescribe the appropriate level of support necessary to meet the challenges of CCSS implementation without a thorough analysis of data that shows the gap between the goals set for where we are headed with CCSS and what it will take for us all to get there.

The range of exposure to a standards-based system in the United States is as diverse as the state systems themselves. What could be designed as an orientation in some places would serve as advanced study in others. The great news is that based upon 20-plus years of readiness for standards implementation, we can now build on lessons learned and what we already know. The troubling news is that no generic checklist or transition plan can accommodate the variance in experience with standards-based education across our nation. We must all be diligent in creating our own authentic action steps that will guide us to the goal of full CCSS implementation.

To apply a technology metaphor, each state and district standards-based GPS navigation system has a different starting point, and different routes and roadways plotted for the journey, but the final destination for all of us will occur during school year 2014–15 when everyone who adopted CCSS arrives ready to be assessed on how productive the initial trip was. No pressure here, right? I am optimistic that as ambitious as this task sounds, we collectively have the tools, the skills, and the knowledge to achieve a high degree of success in meeting this challenge.

In addition to the characteristics of adult learners mentioned above, we do know some essentials about effective professional development. Learning Forward, formerly the National Staff Development Council, has created some thoughtful standards to consider when designing quality staff development experiences that address educational context, content, and process (Learning Forward, 2011). First and foremost we know our ultimate goal is to improve learning for all students. We accomplish this by organizing adults into collaborative learning communities that are inquiry- and problem-based and embedded in the continuous work of instructional improvement. These groups use multiple sources of data to select the learning priorities of both students and adults and monitor their ongoing progress. Research-based strategies and content knowledge that are appropriate to the intended learning goals are implemented and evaluated for their effectiveness in meeting rigorous academic standards, which are then communicated to families and stakeholders. These guidelines help us chunk these considerations into manageable and doable parts.

Specifically, what do we need to consider in planning, delivering, and evaluating the professional development that is focused on the English Language arts and mathematics Common Core? How are we going to integrate this new learning and higher expectations for teachers and students with established practice? We know learning spreads. How are we going to ensure that we begin this ascent prepared and positive that we are capable of completing this transitional journey by 2014?

I am proposing some tried and tested professional development strategies that have been very effective in my experience as a school leader and educational consultant. These suggestions are not as explicit as a recommended treasure hunt exercise through the CCSS document to become familiar with its contents; or an introductory agenda on how to follow the design and organizational features in the ELA and mathematics standards; or how to plan an orientation activity to the appendices and additional resources that CCSS provides. Those specifics should be left to individual sites as they accommodate the varied and diverse needs of group learning. What I am suggesting are substantive methods of professional learning that can be structurally adaptable and can easily focus on areas that will have the greatest impact on ramping up teacher practice and student achievement as we move toward CCSS implementation.

## OPTIONS FOR QUALITY PROFESSIONAL LEARNING

### Action Research

Action research is a strategy for learning more about the intricacies of the teaching and learning process. Teachers decide what questions are important to examine that potentially supply a link between professional practice and student results. A description of the particular student population is created listing special characteristics of the learners in the project. Action research involves collecting, analyzing, and interpreting formative and summative assessment data and then determining some appropriate adult actions to observe and document. The model is based on the belief that teachers have the ability to formulate valid research questions about their own practice and pursue objective answers to these queries. Action research assists teachers in becoming more reflective practitioners and more systematic problem solvers. It is certainly not a substitute for scientific research, but it can be used in tandem with a quantifiable data collection. As Stephen White states in his description of the model, "action research is simply a proactive hunt for a better way" (2011a, p. 150; 2011b, p. 61). A potential CCSS action research question might be: Why does the level of text complexity matter, and how are we going to begin to identify current resource materials that deliver the recommended rigor, quality, and range of student reading at various grade levels and departments?

### Examination of Student Work

Collaboratively examining students' work enables teachers to understand how students think, permitting them to provide appropriate and supportive learning and teaching strategies and resources. Teams identify a clear focus for their conversations and how to reach consensus on what their definitions of proficient and advanced work are expected to be. The most fruitful discussions result from using examples of student work that are varied in composition and quality; for example, graded written work from several students in relation to the same assignment that includes students' explanations of their thinking and justification for their responses. The team then infers the misconceptions represented in students' thinking and how to correct them during the re-teach. The discussions highlight the ways in which teachers can enhance their teaching based on what they have learned about students' understanding of important concepts, content, and skills. A specific CCSS task that is suitable for this strategy would be to collaboratively examine current student work samples against the criteria in the CCSS grade specific standards and reach consensus on exemplars of proficient and advanced work. Use of the student and text benchmarks from ELA Appendices B and C would further illustrate the level of rigor expected from the standards.

## Study Groups

Study groups engage in regularly scheduled collaborative interactions around topics identified by the group as areas of instructional interest or need. This model provides opportunities to critique classroom and school practice. Groups can read and discuss educational research publications in a collaborative and supportive environment, or view online resources that contain pertinent content to inform the work. The study group model can include the entire staff of a school in discovering solutions to common problems or create smaller task-specific teams to work together on a common concern. Opportunities are provided for groups to share their findings and recommendations with other staff members. An example of this model to support discussions about CCSS implementation would be to investigate the vertical and horizontal alignment of the Common Core by examining a particular College and Career Ready (CCR) anchor standard and highlight or underline the new skills and concepts that are added at each grade level.

## Lesson Study

Lesson study is a teaching improvement and knowledge-building process that has its origins in Japanese elementary education. In Japanese lesson study, teachers work in small teams to design, teach, observe, analyze, and refine individual class lessons, called research lessons, or *kenkyuu jugyou*. Nearly all Japanese teachers participate in a lesson study team during the school year. Research lessons are published and widely disseminated throughout the country. In essence, Japanese lesson study is a broad-based, teacher-led system for improving teaching and learning. Every teacher periodically prepares a lesson or unit of study in collaboration with colleagues that demonstrates strategies to achieve a specific goal. A group of teachers observes the lesson being taught and records their observations and insights. Afterwards, the group discusses the lesson's strengths and challenges, asks clarifying questions, and offers suggestions to improve the lesson. This model of professional development allows teachers to refine individual lessons, consult with other teachers, and receive feedback based on colleagues' observations of their classroom practice. Obviously, this professional development strategy would be an excellent way to increase the bank of lessons and units of study that will support CCSS and use the power of peer observation and coaching to improve instructional practice and create a culture of collaboration and professional learning.

## Peer Observation

One of the most effective ways to learn is by observing others, or being observed and receiving specific feedback from that observation. Analyzing and reflecting on this information can be a valuable method of professional growth. The most effective observations are well planned and focus on specific issues or instructional questions, with follow-up to document growth and improvement. Peer to peer observations promote an open and trusting environment where public discussions of teaching are encouraged and supported. Opportunities to model and demonstrate how classroom teachers are increasing the level of thinking and rigor to existing standards-based lessons would support the attitude that we are all producers and consumers of good ideas and that we can collaboratively construct knowledge and build skillfulness by sharing our practice with colleagues. Models of excellence in CCSS implementation should be shared and celebrated through peer observation.

## Data Teams

Continuous improvement is the foundation of effective data-driven decision making and subsequent professional development focus. Data Teams support a dialogue cycle that identifies needed improvements, develops strategies to initiate those improvements, adjusts along the way, and documents lessons learned to inform the next set of improvements. There are many existing processes that systems have embraced to support continuous quality improvement, and the Leadership and Learning Center model is one of the most successful. Data Teams are structured grade-level or department-level teams that examine individual student work generated from common formative assessments. They determine the effectiveness of instructional decisions that have been implemented and offer suggestions for making midcourse modifications if necessary. The use of student and adult performance data is the primary driver for improvement in this model and informs the decision making by the Data Team. It answers the following questions:

- What data do we have?
- What else do we know or need to know?
- What inferences can we make from analyzing the data?

- What instructional interventions will get results?
- How well did we do?

This powerful model of collaboration would be an excellent format for actively and collaboratively engaging in any aspect of CCSS analysis and connecting those expectations to current student performance data in a school or district.

## Instructional Coaching

Instructional coaching aligns with systemwide school improvement efforts, district redesign, leadership development, accountability, and community-centered educational reform. Effective coaching incorporates an array of connected approaches that advocate and promote coherence and focus on the multiple levels of a school system. Effective coaches and coaching structures build instructional and leadership capacity by applying what is known about adult learning and change theory. Coaching supports the systemic improvement efforts of school communities that push beyond individual teacher behavior or even the work of an individual school. Coaching holds the potential to address inequities in opportunities for teacher and student learning by providing differentiated and targeted support. The structures and culture that well-implemented coaching models provide can increase collective responsibility throughout a school system for students and their learning. In cases where coaches are effective liaisons between school practice and district initiatives, emerging evidence shows that they can facilitate professional learning that supports systemwide initiatives more powerfully. Instructional coaching represents a critical professional development support in the CCSS implementation by modeling and demonstrating the expectations for rigor that exist in the new standards for English language arts and mathematics.

## Professional Learning Communities

Richard DuFour and colleagues define a professional learning community as "educators committed to working collaboratively in ongoing processes of collective inquiry and action research to achieve better results for the students they serve. Professional learning communities operate under the assumption that the key to improved learning for students is continuous, job-embedded learning for educators" (DuFour, DuFour, & Eaker, 2008, p. 14). The professional learning community model is a powerful way of working together that profoundly affects the practices of schooling. But initiating and sustaining the concept is hard work. It requires a school staff to focus on learning rather than teaching, work collaboratively on matters related to learning, and hold itself accountable for the kind of results that fuel continual improvement. When educators do the intense work necessary to implement these principles, their collective ability to help all students learn increases. The success of the professional learning community concept depends on the most important element in the improvement of any school—the commitment and persistence of the educators within it.

The above-mentioned professional development models present some research-based best practices in providing high-quality and powerful adult learning experiences that will support CCSS implementation. The proclivity we share as American educators is to look for quick fixes or shortcuts to results. To avoid this tendency, rather than offer very finite and specific professional development activities, I recommend these collective strategies for accomplishing the heavy lifting and the active work that is necessary to improve instructional practice.

## FROM COMMON SENSE TO COMMON PRACTICE IN PROFESSIONAL DEVELOPMENT

The appearance of the Common Core and its apparent acceptance by the majority of states creates the need to attend to the issue of its reception, interpretation, and implementation by our nation's educators. This issue cuts both ways. On the one hand, teachers need to be supported and encouraged as they take ownership of CCSS and its implications for curriculum development and classroom practice. On the other hand, teachers and educators will collectively need to mediate the differences in content emphases and norms of practice that will inevitably emerge if the Common Core is to become a framework for learning with all of our students.

Common Core State Standards present an excellent opportunity for the teaching community to advance its own professionalism. One of the explicit goals would be the establishment of norms for professional excellence that are generated and maintained primarily from within the profession itself. This is typical in most professions in our society currently. This will not occur in a day, or, on a large scale, even in a decade. But the call that gave birth to the Common Core State Standards for students can create a realistic prospect to do the same for our teachers and administrators.

We know how to nurture professional development in our teachers, to support them as they develop their skillfulness and competence. This chapter has offered several different types of job-embedded and ongoing experiences that honor the tenets of adult learning theory and offer opportunities for self-renewal and professional growth that are necessary for the successful implementation of CCSS.

## DO THIS NOW, DO THIS NEXT, AND DO THIS LATER

### Now . . .

Determine through an extensive needs assessment what content and pedagogical supports are necessary for teachers to feel confident and competent with CCSS implementation and use that list to identify some options to deliver job-embedded and ongoing professional development training.

Begin to look closely at current student work as a collaborative team to determine the obvious next steps to reach Common Core rigor in English language arts and mathematics.

Engage all students in at least one ELA task such as reading and analyzing informational text and writing to state an opinion or argument and one mathematics task aligned to a strategically selected CCSS for mathematics and closely analyze the resulting student work each quarter.

### Next . . .

Using some of the professional development strategies in this chapter, deepen efforts to engage teachers in the next stages of alignment of curriculum and assessment to CCSS.

Create reading and writing progressions that indicate the number of short texts and full-length books that meet the requirements of CCSS, as well as the percentage of time needed to write about analytical and narrative materials.

Begin increasing argumentative writing across all areas of the curriculum and at every level.

### Later . . .

Continue to engage all students in rigorous tasks embedded in well-crafted instructional units with appropriate adult and student supports.

Begin the challenging discussion about how to support all learners through differentiation of instruction and assessment.

Using short cycles of frequent and focused classrooms observations, school leaders can begin creating a common lens to identify effective instruction and provide specific feedback to teachers to enhance their practice. Charlotte Danielson's *Enhancing Professional Practice: A Framework for Teaching* (2007) is an excellent resource to inform this work.

## KEY IDEAS FOR CHAPTER 6

→ Professional learning experiences for adults must be meaningful, relevant, engaging, and sustainable.

→ We need to be deliberate and thoughtful in our assessment and evaluation of effective professional development opportunities.

→ Adults appreciate personal choice and individual control and respond positively to activities that support accomplishing their work more efficiently and effectively.

→ The ultimate goal of professional development experiences is improved student learning, and we as teachers need to be ever mindful of that responsibility and challenge.

→ There are many job-embedded options for ongoing professional development that can provide support for adult learning.

→ The implementation of CCSS offers an excellent opportunity to enhance the professionalism of our educational system as we advance our vital work.

## QUESTIONS TO CONTINUE THIS DISCUSSION

☑ How is professional development perceived as a part of the ongoing work in education?

☑ How can the need for both individual growth and organizational development be satisfied within the same professional development opportunities?

☑ How can the knowledge and skillfulness of excellent teaching be collectively represented so that others can retrieve it, understand it, and replicate it?

☑ How can effective professional development be assessed and evaluated?

☑ What specific professional development strategies meet the criteria of being job-embedded and sustainable in your educational context?

☑ How can the structures of professional learning communities support collaboratively examining student work and planning for effective instruction?

# Next-Generation Assessment Systems

*Not everything that can be counted counts,
and not everything that counts can be counted.*

—Albert Einstein

**M**any educators refer to this quote by Albert Einstein when describing the challenges and frustrations they feel toward high-stakes standardized testing and its impact on day-to-day teaching and learning. Teachers often complain how testing can narrow the curriculum, limit the variety of student learning opportunities, emphasize only basic skills, and fail to measure higher-level thinking. Teachers feel that they support students in learning so much more than what is reflected on test scores. The majority of teachers do not teach in subjects and grade levels that are tested at the state level, but they feel the pressure to side with colleagues who do.

Indeed, we are living and working in an era of transparency as educators. In the face of increased scrutiny about our teaching effectiveness, expanded demands for providing educational quality, and unparalleled consequences for failure to deliver what we and our students are expected to accomplish, we sometimes feel overexamined and underappreciated. In other words, we are constantly being "sized up" by our stakeholders, sometimes fairly and at other times unfairly. How we fare in this public evaluation is determined largely by what measurements and agendas are deemed important to assess our performance and how these results are benchmarked against an arbitrary standard. This test of our professionalism certainly has the potential to leave us cynical and disheartened, but if done right, it can serve as validation of our efforts.

Education International General Secretary Fred van Leeuwen comes to our defense at the first International Summit on the Teaching Profession held in New York City on March 16, 2011, by stating that "teachers are not against testing. We invented it. However, we consider testing as a teachers' diagnostic tool, not a political device." He argued for the need to "rely on evidence-based strategies that strengthen the system as a whole, not experiment with competitive programs designed to create a few winners and many losers" (van Leeuwen, 2011). We need a new attitude toward assessment. No Child Left Behind has placed a sour taste in our mouths by taking testing to an elevated position of political power and influence, and the aftermath has left us skeptical about the entire assessment process. We need to return to the primary goal of assessing students to support their learning and inform our instructional practices, not to sort and select winners and losers in the achievement game. Assessment must be refocused on becoming an integral part of good teaching again, revealing what students know and can do, the learning strategies they use, the depth of understanding they bring to their personal learning, and how to inform our instructional decisions to assist in moving our students forward. Teachers and parents use test scores to gauge a student's academic strengths and weaknesses, communities rely on these scores to judge the quality of their educational system, and state and federal lawmakers use these same metrics to determine whether schools are meeting their obligations to the public. We need to get the assessment obligation back on track for everyone's sake.

## LESSONS OLD AND NEW ABOUT ASSESSMENT SYSTEMS

The reality is that assessment information is gathered for many different purposes and for many diverse publics, and therein lies the design challenge. Some stakeholders value snapshots of what students know and can do at prescribed times in their educational careers for accountability reasons. Others view data as a means to evaluate teachers and schools systematically. For some, the main system goal is to collect actionable data that can be used to improve instructional planning for the benefit of all students, while others see assessment as an auditing or return on investment strategy to evaluate the impact of certain initiatives and programs. Most agree that formal summative assessments should be as short and as inexpensive as possible to administer and score, but some would compromise speed and cost to obtain more authentic and complex results from standards-based performance tasks. Some see the advantage of comparing state-to-state results and others insist on local control over the content of assessments. All of these contradictory views complicate the simplicity of just testing to see where our students are in their learning at a given point in time.

American educators stand at a crossroads of unprecedented opportunity to transform assessment into a legitimate, fair, and accurate system that measures the results of our work in Common Core State Standards with reliability and validity. However, with this opportunity comes risk. The decisions we make now may well affect the course of assessment efforts in the United States for years to come. We must be very thoughtful and deliberate about how we approach the work of creating authentic and practical assessment tools that align with CCSS.

Advances in technology, together with innovative assessment task design and sophisticated psychometric models, make it more plausible than ever before to obtain a richer, more intelligent, and more nuanced picture of what our students know and can do. While this historic opportunity to change the direction of education is real, so are the challenges inherent in any change in the assessment paradigm. No single test, not even an integrated assessment system, can adequately serve all of the educational purposes and satisfy every patron's expectations for relevant achievement information. Any assessment structure represents a compromise between competing and conflicting priorities. It will be difficult to address both the accountability and the instructional demands in a next-generation assessment system, but we need to reach consensus on a shared vision that is comprehensive and realistic or we miss a tremendous opportunity to improve education as a whole.

Considerations for driving this assessment initiative should include

- Full alignment with the Common Core State Standards and a robust and sophisticated array of test items and performance tasks that measure domain proficiency through the breadth and depth of the knowledge and skills described in the standards
- A wide range of data collection methods that support decision making at all levels: student readiness for college and career, student growth over time, and benchmarks for comparative achievement against the standards
- Formative or interim assessments that inform, support, and improve classroom instruction
- Coherent and integrated systems that accurately measure with intention the summative requirements of the standards, in grades 3–8 and high school
- Cross-state collaboration to ensure comparability of summative results and to create the potential to promote cost efficiency by

employing economies of scale for research and development, and administration and scoring

- Flexibility to assess the 15% optional augmented core to measure state-specific information
- Technology-based open-source solutions for more effective and efficient delivery and scoring of state assessments and streamlined reporting of the results for accountability and instructional decision making
- Necessary accommodations for special student populations to support full access and participation in the assessment system
- Opportunities for classroom teachers to become more literate in assessment and involved in the process of designing and evaluating appropriate assessment experiences for their students (U.S. Department of Education, 2009)

## TWO CONSORTIA WILL POTENTIALLY PROVIDE THE ANSWERS

Groups of 15 or more states were encouraged to collectively apply for a combined federal grant to design, develop, and pilot a next-generation, multilayered assessment system with the following requirements (U.S. Department of Education, 2009):

- Must include the ability to assess the acquisition of the breadth and depth of the content and skills represented in the Common Core State Standards and measure progress toward college and career readiness by the completion of high school
- Must include common and comparable scores across member states of the consortium
- Must provide student achievement and student growth information for teacher and principal evaluation and professional development
- Must assess all students, except those with "significant cognitive difficulties"
- Must be sensitive to the technological demands, challenges, and capacities to administer online assessments and endorse timely scoring of the results for use in instructional planning
- Must use multiple types of test items and performance tasks to gain a more valid and richer measure of what students know and can do meeting the CCSS in English language arts and mathematics

States were given a momentous chance in 2010 to compete for substantial Race to the Top funds to create next-generation assessment systems that would better fulfill the many purposes inherent in assessment programs: providing rich summative data that could guide decision making while also informing and inspiring high-quality daily instruction in classrooms. The next generation of state assessments is necessary to make the Common Core State Standards concrete and meaningful to educators, students, and parents and to provide a critical process for ensuring that all students master essential knowledge and skills in the content areas of English language arts and mathematics. This initiative is about much more than creating better tests. It is intended to produce a timelier and more comprehensive data set that improves instruction, accelerates learning, and provides essential information about how our schools and our students are performing based upon the CCSS adopted in 46 states and Washington, D.C. A huge challenge, right?

Recognizing the critical importance to support this bold federal funding opportunity, the Council of Chief State School Officers (CCSSO) and the National Governors Association (NGA) Center convened in February 2010 for a series of conversations with the leaders of six overlapping state consortia that had already formed to apply for these Race to the Top funds. Participants explored key priorities and the blueprints driving each consortium and identified areas of consensus that would provide a foundation for common action. Those discussions yielded important agreements that would greatly facilitate collaboration to improve the quality, cost-effectiveness, and comparability of the new state assessments. Leaders of the six initial consortia agreed to

- Embrace a common vision for assessment
- Develop a list of shared priorities for leveraging Race to the Top funds to design next-generation assessment systems
- Merge their efforts considerably to reduce the number of consortia moving forward with written proposals
- Participate in a joint NGA-CCSSO project to ensure comparability of summative assessment results across the consortia and to reduce costs by collaborating on other activities that require extensive funding

On September 2, 2010, the U.S. Department of Education announced the winners of the Race to the Top Comprehensive Assessment Systems Competition. The Partnership for the Assessment of Readiness for College and Careers (PARCC; 2010) and the SMARTER Balanced Assessment Consortium (SBAC; 2010) were selected as the two proposals that met all of the criteria outlined in the federal application guidelines. Designed to replace the patchwork and disparate state tests in English language arts and mathematics currently mandated by the No Child Left Behind Act, the PARCC and SBAC assessment systems are to launch an innovative approach to assessment design that will complement the adoption and implementation of the Common Core State Standards. These new standards and the aligned assessments have significant implications for how states and districts organize and support efforts to improve student achievement in English language arts and mathematics.

Both consortia, which include all but four states, initially received more than $330 million in Race to the Top grant monies to design two reliable and affordable assessment options that are aligned to the Common Core, are of the highest quality, are compatible with curriculum and instruction as well as accountability purposes, test 21st century skills, and are flexibly built to accommodate online and interactive technology. And, if those criteria are not complex and ambitious enough, they both later expanded their roles to include providing curriculum resources and instructional materials to teachers and the necessary professional development to implement the entire system of assessment requirements. Each state consortium received an additional $16 million to support these supplementary responsibilities.

By the 2014–2015 school year, for the first time in the history of American education, the daily work of teachers in PARCC and SBAC states will be driven by common standards and common assessments designed to prepare all students for success in college and careers. Participating states and districts will build a next-generation governance infrastructure to ensure that school-based professionals have the resources they need to take full advantage of the PARCC and SBAC assessment systems.

Though similar in many respects, both consortia emphasize a different set of priorities. As a result, there are at least four important distinctions between the PARCC and SBAC approaches to system design that warrant a closer examination of the two proposals. With regard to summative assessments, PARCC envisions a "through-course" model of summative assessment for accountability, which will require participating states to administer quarterly assessments in both ELA and mathematics. Each of these quarterly assessments will be added together to obtain summative scores for accountability determinations. SBAC adheres to a more traditional "end-of-year" approach, with summative assessments administered during the last 12 weeks of the school year. High school assessments are also dealt with differently. PARCC requires tests in grades 9–11, while SBAC requires testing only once in high school, during the 11th grade. The SBAC will develop optional assessments for grades 9 and 10. SBAC assessments will be computer-adaptive, which is a method of test administration that adjusts in real time the assessment's level of difficulty based on individual students' responses. PARCC assessments will be computer-based but adhere to a single test form for all students. SBAC will set initial cut scores in the summer of 2014, following the field testing of its assessments but before the first full-scale administration of the assessment system in all consortium states. Alternatively, PARCC will finalize assessment standards and set cut scores only after full-scale administration during the 2014–2015 school year.

A deeper look at each consortium is warranted to compare and contrast the finer points of the vision and blueprint of each.

## SMARTER Balanced Assessment Consortium (SBAC)

Initially, three independent groups—SMARTER, MOSAIC, and a team focused on creating balanced and integrated testing materials led by Linda Darling-Hammond—worked on separate applications for the Race to the Top monies that would fund the development of a set of innovative assessments aligned to the Common Core State Standards for grades 3–8 and high school. Realizing that their visions and goals were very similar, they merged and wrote one comprehensive proposal that was approved for four years and awarded $175.8 million.

The SBAC of 29 states, 18 governing (decision-making and only part of this consortium) and 11 advisory (informational and can be part of both consortia), representing over 20 million of the nation's K–12 students, set priorities for a new-generation assessment system that is rooted in shared beliefs that assessment must support ongoing improvements in instruction and learning, and must include useful information for all members of the educational enterprise: students, parents, teachers, school administrators, members of the general public, and policy makers. The consortium recognizes the need for a system of both formative and summative assessments organized around CCSS that supports high-quality learning and also the demands of accountability, and that balances concern for innovative assessment design with the need for a fiscally sustainable system that is feasible and practical for states to implement.

The goal of the SBAC is to ensure that all students leave high school prepared for postsecondary success in college or a career through increased student learning and improved teaching. The theory of action or model of the milestones to accomplish this is grounded in a thoughtful standards-based curriculum and represents an integrated system of assessments that produces valid and reliable evidence of student performance. Teachers are involved in the development process and scoring of these multiple assessment measures that are committed to improved teaching and learning.

To that end, the SBAC system highlights include

- Summative assessments administered during the last 12 weeks of the school year that
  - Utilize online computer adaptive technologies that can assess the full rigor and range of CCSS in English language arts and mathematics
  - Incorporate adaptive precision into performance tasks and events
  - Show current mastery of the CCSS as well as growth over time toward college and career readiness
  - Provide scores for state-to-state comparability
  - Provide the opportunity to take the summative exam twice during the school year

- Optional interim assessments benchmarked during instruction as progress checks that
  - Are aligned to the summative assessments and provide an on-track trajectory for success
  - Identify specific student instructional needs that can be addressed in differentiated classroom instruction
  - Incorporate significant teacher involvement in the design and scoring of items and tasks
  - Are nonsecure and fully accessible for use in instruction and professional development activities
  - Provide clear examples of expected student performance on the CCSS

- A digital library of formative tools, processes, and practices that support improved teaching and student learning by providing frequent opportunities to monitor and adjust instruction based on the interim assessment results
- Open-source technology that is collaboratively developed and available free to all participating member states
- Computer adaptive technology that allows items to be presented as a function of student ability measured during the actual testing situation to minimize the test length
- A reporting system that is online, provides information about student progress toward college and career readiness, and allows an exchange of student performance history across districts and states
- Economies of scale that provide cost savings, shared item generation and banking, and common protocols for accommodating special needs students

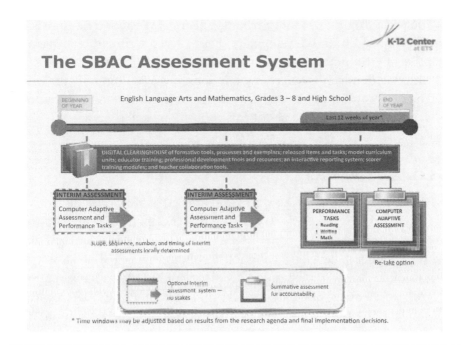

**Exhibit 7.1**   ETS SBAC Illustration

This graphical illustration of the Smarter Balanced Assessment Consortium was developed by the K-12 Center at ETS and approved for accuracy by the consortium. July 2011 www .k12center.org

## SBAC Implementation Milestones

| 2011–2012 | Develop, procure, and review materials to populate the digital library |
| | Develop test specifications and test blueprints for summative assessments; vet state-submitted items and tasks and determine procurement needs |
| | Develop sample item/task sets and initial achievement level descriptors |
| 2012–2013 | Develop exemplar modules of formative assessment tasks and tools and PD modules; conduct teacher training |
| | Pilot test items and tasks |
| 2013–2014 | Conduct field test of items and tasks |
| 2015 | Administer summative assessments; verify and adopt final achievement level standards |

**Exhibit 7.2**   ETS SBAC Timeline

This graphical illustration of the Smarter Balanced Assessment Consortium was developed by the K-12 Center at ETS and approved for accuracy by the consortium. July 2011 www .k12center.org

The project management partner for SBAC is WestEd, a nonpartisan, nonprofit, research and development–based service educational agency. Linda Darling-Hammond serves as the senior research adviser to the consortium, Sue Gendron is the policy adviser, and Washington State is the fiscal agent. Visit http://www.k12.wa.us/smarter for much more discrete and descriptive information about this consortium's plan and work.

## Partnership for Assessment of Readiness for College and Careers (PARCC)

PARCC is an alliance of 26 states and the District of Columbia, including 15 governing states and 11 advisory or participating states, that represents over 31 million of America's K–12 students. This consortium is working together to develop a common set of assessments that are aligned to the Common Core State Standards and are anchored in what is required to be ready for college and careers after high school. PARCC was awarded $186 million in funding for the four-year duration of the Race to the Top grant.

The purpose of the PARCC proposal is to increase the rates at which students graduate from high school prepared for success in college and the workplace. Their theory of action that supports this work is based upon the intention that the assessments will provide a wider range of data that is useful for analyzing effectiveness, calibrating instructional interventions, presenting accountability results, and identifying professional development and support needs for educators. One distinctive difference in the PARCC proposal is that it involves more than 200 institutions of higher learning to help with the development of the high school exit assessments.

The PARCC system design highlights include

- Only summative assessments, which are intended to be administered four times throughout the school year closer to the actual time of instruction and are
  - Labeled through-course assessments, which allow for midyear monitoring and adjustments to instruction
  - Administered near the end of the first, second, and third quarters and at the end of the school year in grades 3–8, and once in high school, and are scored and reported cumulatively
  - Administered online and available as open-source technology using a variety of item types to measure the full range of CCSS in English language arts and mathematics

- o Used to inform both instructional decision making and for accountability purposes
  - o Reporting results online to all stakeholders that support cross-state comparisons

- The Partnership Resource Center, a web-based platform that houses a collection of resources for teachers, students, administrators, and parents and provides
  - o Shared model curricular frameworks, units of study, exemplar lessons plans, and sample assessment tasks that support CCSS
  - o Released test items and performance tasks for use in instruction
  - o Professional development modules for training in understanding the assessment system, how to implement the assessments, and how to interpret and use the results
  - o Online practice tests for teachers and students
  - o A portal for teachers to create and share a bank of innovative formative assessment items and performance tasks

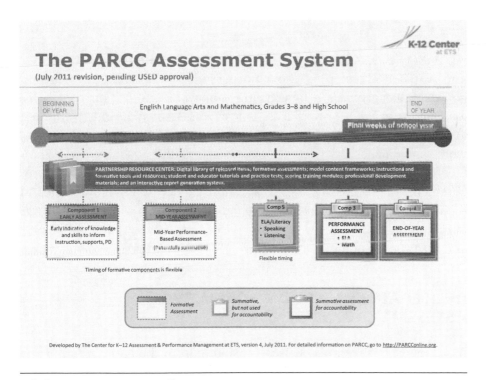

**Exhibit 7.3**     ETS PARCC Illustration

This graphical illustration of the PARCC Assessment Consortium was developed by the K-12 Center at ETS and approved for accuracy by the consortium. July 2011 www.k12center.org

## PARCC Implementation Milestones

| 2011–2012 | Item and task development, piloting of components |
| --- | --- |
| | Release of Model Content Frameworks and prototype items and tasks |
| | Development of professional development resources and online platform |
| 2012–2014 | Field testing |
| 2014–2015 | New summative assessments in use |
| Summer 2015 | Setting of common achievement standards |

**Exhibit 7.4**      ETS PARCC Timeline

This graphical illustration of the PARCC Assessment Consortium was developed by the K-12 Center at ETS and approved for accuracy by the consortium. July 2011 www .k12center.org

PARCC selected Achieve Inc. as its project management partner and Mitchell Chester as the chairperson of the PARCC governing board. Achieve Inc. is a bipartisan, nonprofit organization that helps states raise academic standards, improve assessments, and strengthen accountability to prepare all young people for postsecondary education, work, and citizenship. The nation's governors and business leaders created it in 1996 following the first National Education Summit. The procurement state is Florida, which is responsible for all fiscal auditing and reporting. Additional information about this consortium's work can be found online (http://www.fldoe.org/parcc, http://www.parcconline.org, and http://www.achieve.org/parcc).

## DELIBERATE CLASSROOM FORMATIVE ASSESSMENT: A MUST

Assessment, in the purest sense, translating from the Latin origin of the word, *assidere,* means to "sit beside" one who is a novice at learning a new skill or piece of knowledge to give feedback to improve and get better—to coach on what is going well and what still needs work. That definition should guide our efforts at refocusing the critical role assessment has in improved learning.

Most assessment experts, including Richard Stiggins, James Popham, and Grant Wiggins, share the belief that classroom formative assessments are the most valuable form of testing to improve student learning. Specifically, they advocate for an assessment system that goes far beyond fulfilling a simple accountability function by documenting what students have achieved, which is commonly known as assessments "of" learning. In addition, they request assessments that inform how to plan instruction, noted as assessments "for" learning, and most important, engaging students and teachers in worthwhile educational experiences in and of themselves that are labeled assessments "as" learning. Both consortia agree with these leaders in the psychometric field that a formal method for collecting ongoing data about student performance is a necessary process to ensure that the students are on target for success on the high-stakes summative measures of achievement. This is good news for all of us that deliberate and informed help is finally coming in creating assessments "of" learning, "for" learning, and "as" learning.

According to Dylan Wiliam in his article "Changing Classroom Practice" (2007–2008), to tap the full potential of formative assessments, teachers must

- Clarify and share learning intentions and criteria for success with students. For example, some teachers share work samples completed by previous students and have current students discuss which ones are strong and which are weak, and why.
- Engineer effective classroom discussions, questions, and learning tasks. Well-planned questions can prompt students to think and provide teachers with information to adjust instruction. Teachers need to use effective questioning techniques that keep all students engaged and that gauge the understanding of the whole class instead of just selected students.
- Provide feedback that moves learners forward. Comments that address what the student needs to do to improve, linked to rubrics when appropriate, promote further learning more effectively than letter grades do.
- Activate students as the owners of their own learning. For example, have students assess their own work, using agreed-on criteria for success.
- Encourage students to be instructional resources for one another. Peer assessment and feedback is often more acceptable and engaging for students than teacher feedback is.

Wiliam (2007–2008) also states that evidence from 4,000 research studies conducted over a 40-year period indicates that "well implemented formative assessments can effectively double the speed of student learning."

And if these endorsements are not convincing enough, W. Edwards Deming, American consultant, statistician, and educator, stated, "Quality is the result of regular inspections along the way" (in McTighe, 1996/1997). Periodic checks are more important to ensuring good work than the end measurement. What you do in terms of assessment should in the long run always help students learn better and help teachers teach better. Assessments "of" learning for accountability purposes and program evaluation place second to the primary function of assessments "for" and "as" learning to improve student achievement.

I believe enhanced learning is based on that same regular and ongoing progress monitoring that Deming and others suggest. Students learn in incremental steps. Students need time and opportunity to practice, to clarify, and to refine their thinking based upon specific feedback from the teacher. The Linda Darling-Hammond quote, "You don't fatten the cattle by weighing them" (in McTighe, 1996/1997), or Richard Stiggins's similar statement, "Stepping on the scale doesn't make your weight change" (ASCD, 1997), indicate that nothing positive happens if you just take a measurement and do not act on the resultant information.

CCSS ensures that we will be assessing what we collectively value and deem important, but we must take that one step further so that we value what we assess and discover its usefulness in our improvement efforts. It follows that what is inspected is expected and what is expected is inspected. Linda Darling-Hammond's research presented in *The Right to Learn: A Blueprint for Creating Schools That Work* (1997) reveals that in every successful school she observed, which were hundreds by the way, systems were in place to know their students well and act on that knowledge. The 90/90/90 schools that Douglas Reeves (2010) mentions in his research supports this point as well, that the information gained from assessments must be used formatively to guide instructional decisions to improve student learning. That is why the student should be the primary beneficiary of any data that is collected, summative or formative.

## PERFORMANCE TASKS TO PROMOTE LEARNING

Grant Wiggins (1998), in *Educative Assessment,* spends an entire chapter discussing how to promote student understanding. He argues that understanding is personal and difficult to assess without sophisticated performance tasks that require students to regularly rethink what they thought they understood. When the task is real world and applies to an audience outside of the classroom, the work for the students becomes challenging and exciting. Students who thoroughly understand a concept can

- Explain it
- Predict it
- Apply or adapt it
- Demonstrate it
- Verify, defend, or justify it
- Connect it

And isn't that the definition of learning? Wouldn't we be excited as teachers to see that thorough understanding evidenced in students' eyes on a daily basis? Wouldn't that alone motivate us to create active and engaging tasks for students to demonstrate their depth of understanding in what they know and can do relative to the CCSS?

What I have learned over the years is that what students do with what we as teachers provide them is a function of how they interpret the value of what we offer. Meaning is not randomly distributed; it is personally created. Assessments that provide evidence about what a student knows and is able to do in real, not proxy, situations give us the information we need to make judgments about where students are in relationship to the standards and what our next instructional steps should be. This is the purpose of formative assessment and will become a powerful and essential consideration in the successful implementation of CCSS.

Whether we teach primary students or high school science or language arts in a rural or urban setting, we all work toward effectively teaching two things: knowledge and know-how, content and skills, or as mentioned in a previous chapter, declarative and procedural knowledge. We need to become expert at measuring how well we are teaching these two types of knowledge before student achievement improves substantially. Our next-generation assessment system must emphasize the significance of knowing our learners well in many contexts and situations that mirror authentic and real-world applications to ensure that we are collecting reliable and valid data on their performance.

There are currently over 3 million Internet sites that address some aspect of performance assessments. At its best, a performance assessment

- Is open, not secret, and clearly communicates the expectations and procedures of the task and provides a clear target at which to aim

- Is designed so that a large number of students, and ideally every student, can achieve proficiency given time and instructional opportunity, not just the 49.9% on right side of the bell curve
- Involves a demonstration of performance proficiency, not just a lucky guess on a multiple-choice test
- Expects students to demonstrate higher-order thinking to analyze, evaluate, estimate, simplify, convert, and organize new information
- Teaches the criteria and expectations for meeting success as a part of the assessment
- Highlights elements of quality as well as illustrating how the work will be evaluated

You can see that these characteristics of a quality performance assessment automatically are more equitable and achievable, and have the potential to be more motivating for students and more informative for teachers. The authors of the assessment systems being designed by SBAC and PARCC have heeded this advice and plan to incorporate opportunities for students to engage in interim or formative performance events as a part of their recommended proposals.

Authentic, demonstrable, meaningful, and rigorous are the key words in any discussion or description that amplifies the differences between a traditional norm-referenced test, which sorts and selects, and a performance-based test, which is based upon criteria and connects what is required to the real world. Thoughtful work in designing performance tasks should guarantee students

- Worthwhile intellectual problems that are validated against real-world problems, roles, and situations
- Clear, consistent, fair, published standards for evaluating student work and examples of excellent models available for students to emulate
- No secrecy or "gotcha" mentality by the creators of the tasks
- Opportunities to rework and resubmit assignments based upon genuine and helpful feedback
- Choices of ways to demonstrate proficiency to incorporate learning strengths
- Policies that acknowledge the need for a balance between high-stakes testing and formative classroom assessments

Richard Stiggins (2005) encourages us to rethink the relationship between assessment and motivation. If students don't want to learn, they won't; and if they don't feel able to learn, they can't. It is their positive atti-tude and focused effort that supports their journey to success. Remember in Chapter 1, our discussion about mindsets? The same principles apply here. When assessment is a legitimate part of the teaching and learning cycle, students become more self-directed and more self-critical, and as a result they become experts in guiding their own learning, which should be a valued goal of instruction.

We learn limited information the first time it is introduced to us. Learners must have time and opportunity to reflect, reconsider, rethink, and revise based upon their own background and experience with the concept. That takes time and coaching. Learners need gentle opportuni-ties for practice with a new skill or piece of knowledge before they are asked to demonstrate mastery of it. David Perkins (1993), from Harvard University, calls this "fragile knowledge." Students are not able to apply it until the concept becomes a solid part of their individual schema or experiential base.

We learn to do something complex through careful guidance and receiving and using accurate feedback. Piano lessons, T-ball for 6-year-olds, and learning to read, to write, and to compute all follow this premise. Learning to ride a bike begins with a Big Wheel, a tricycle, then with training wheels, and finally a two-wheeler. The delicate bal-ance of the right amount of support and challenge is what teachers seek every day in the classroom, and accurate assessment helps pro-vide that equation.

Mike Schmoker recommends that educators look at their weakest students to determine how effective their school is. Exemplary schools have a smaller achievement gap between their best and worst-performing students. Exemplary schools pay attention to how members in subgroups perform and try to reduce the performance differences among those sub-groups. Before this sophisticated analysis can happen, schools must agree on what proficiency means for their children. Teachers who determine the ranges of possible quality and agree on what proficient and advanced work looks like must anchor and benchmark student work samples. This consensus gives power and ownership to the students and focus and align-ment to the teachers and parents.

This work of standards and assessments is difficult. We get tired, disillusioned, and downright cranky sometimes. However, if we keep our eye on the prize, which is in our case improved student achievement, the rewards are worth every late night, every debate with a colleague, and every parent or community challenge. Students will let us know we are on the right track by their excitement about learning and their willingness to raise their own bar in collaboration with us.

## FROM COMMON SENSE TO COMMON PRACTICE IN NEXT-GENERATION ASSESSMENT SYSTEMS

Do we agree that we want to be better next year than we are today? Do we agree that every single one of us can be better with enhanced levels of knowledge and skills? Do we agree that our students will benefit if we make better teaching and leadership decisions based upon accurate and timely data? Do we agree that we have a lot of work to do in the area of next-generation assessment systems and the time is now for us to take charge of this critical aspect of educational reform? Of course, the obvious answer to each of these questions is yes. The argument is not about needing new and better assessment systems; it is about how those next-generation measurements should be designed so that we receive actionable information that better reflects how our students are doing relative to the CCSS.

Tests should teach in addition to measure. Both assessment consortia recognize this distinction and appreciate what that belief implies in item and task design. There are some very exciting benefits of common assessments proposed by SBAC and PARCC that have the potential to dramatically improve education. First of all, they provide a common and consistent measure that will allow states the opportunity to compare student performance on a common metric. Second, better aligned assessments, teaching resources, and innovations in research and technology can be developed and leveraged at a reduced cost to each state by pooling financial and intellectual talent that is working toward a common goal. Increased collaboration across state boundaries will enhance the quality of curriculum materials, formative assessments, instructional tools, and professional development.

As the two assessment consortia work to guarantee that the next generation of assessments provides instructionally useful information to schools, teachers, parents, and most important, students, it will be critical to plan training on how to utilize and maximize the data collection that is generated from the new assessments. Additionally, during the evolution of the next-generation assessment systems that are designed to measure the more rigorous and robust standards and skills in the CCSS, it will be necessary to focus on professional development in the English language arts and mathematics content areas to reflect the research-based instructional strategies that improve academic achievement. The prospects are exciting.

## DO THIS NOW, DO THIS NEXT, AND DO THIS LATER

### Now . . .

Start by modeling and guiding the process for prioritizing standards in targeted content areas. An excellent resource to support this work is *Rigorous Curriculum Design: How to Create Curriculum Units of Study That Align Standards, Instruction, and Assessment,* by Larry Ainsworth (2010).

Practice unwrapping a CCSS standard to visually illustrate what students are to know and be able to do with a grade-level or content-based expectation. Again, you can use the Ainsworth book to guide this process.

Practice writing big ideas and essential questions using a CCSS ELA or mathematics standard that focuses the instruction on what the explicit core concept is and how students will demonstrate mastery of the standard.

### Next . . .

Create a basic scoring guide for writing that can be used with performance tasks or assessments to determine the level of writing proficiency displayed by students.

Collaboratively create an engaging performance assessment that demonstrates the knowledge and skills required of students with one ELA or mathematics standard.

Begin evaluating student results in collaborative groups to discover learning strengths and areas of concern.

### Later . . .

Engage in discussions about the concept of assessment literacy and how teachers' skillfulness in this area can be enhanced through quality professional development opportunities.

Explore websites that offer current information about the progress of the PARCC and SBAC assessment work and discuss the implications with colleagues.

Through Professional Learning Communities or another collaborative structure, revisit the effectiveness of the current assessment efforts in your school or district compared with some of the suggestions offered in this chapter.

## KEY IDEAS FOR CHAPTER 7

→ Educators need to embrace a new trust and sense of hope toward the next generation of richer and more authentic assessments, which will be designed to inform, not just audit, student learning.

→ The SMARTER Balanced Assessment Consortium and the Partnership for the Assessment of College and Career Readiness are both committed to creating a thoughtful, authentic, and valid system of measuring student performance.

→ Tests should both teach and measure.

→ Both formative and summative assessments should be provided in a balanced system because they have different purposes.

→ Formative assessments have the potential to dramatically increase student learning.

→ Performance tasks reveal what students know and can do with much more depth and accuracy than the typical norm-referenced test.

## QUESTIONS TO CONTINUE THIS DISCUSSION

☑ How are we going to increase the competence and confidence of educators, sometimes called assessment literacy, in implementing and using a new and more comprehensive assessment system?

☑ How are the implications of a sophisticated and rigorous assessment system going to reach each classroom and ultimately each student?

☑ How can formatively designed performance tasks be incorporated into a robust assessment system?

☑ How are educators going to have deliberate and productive opportunities to learn more about the PARCC and SBAC approaches to assessment?

# Powerful Learning Through Powerful Technology

*What we want is to see the child in pursuit of knowledge, and not knowledge in pursuit of the child.*

—George Bernard Shaw

When it comes to the topic of this chapter, technology in our schools, I am an old dog desperately trying to learn new tricks. My own children and grandchildren, highly proficient interacting with anything that has a cable or an app, laugh at my naive questions, my fright at potentially losing a piece of revised and edited text somewhere in cyberspace, and the repetition of instructions necessary to get me moving past the power button. I am truly a novice learner when it comes to technology, and I am constantly reminded of how it feels to lack information and skills and the diminished feeling of power and control that accompany that limited knowledge. Marc Prensky (2010), who first coined the terms "digital native" and "digital immigrant," needs to meet me and others like me of the "baby boomer" generation to label a third group of technology-challenged learners. Our excuses for this lack of technological savvy are often limited time or inclination, but really it is an extreme sense of intimidation that motivates our unwillingness to be pushed, pulled, or dragged into the 21st century digital era. Many adults in education can relate to this.

Today we do almost everything with a computer. Even a greenhorn like myself tweets, chats, researches, writes, shops, Skypes, watches YouTube, and listens to iTunes with the help of my computer. The tragic thing is that there is prolific electronic content and digital interactivity everywhere but in most of our schools. Many students believe that more learning takes places outside of the brick-and-mortar institutions: They suspend their expectations of learning something valuable and authentic until the final bell rings at the end of their formal school day when they are once again allowed to turn on all of their mobile electronic devices.

Even in my innocence, I believe technology can become an important driver for educational change. Integrative technology offers unprecedented opportunities for enhanced performance, adaptability, and cost-effectiveness to any system it supports. Technology can enable a transformation in education but only if educators, parents, policy makers, and the community at large commit to the changes it will bring to our entire system, not just to the classroom.

Currently, students come to school with mobile devices that let them carry the Internet in their pockets or backpacks and allow them to search the Web for information and even answers to test questions. While such behavior in my day was regarded as cheating, now we would be remiss if we did not take advantage of the ever-present access to instantaneous knowledge and resources. A quick swipe of an iPad connects you to limitless information that can be evaluated and shared, enables you to create and present multimedia content to audiences, and allows you to globally interact and collaborate with online social networks and learning communities. The Kaiser Family Foundation discovered in a 2010 survey that children ages 8 to 18 devote an average of 7 hours and 38 minutes to using entertainment media in one day, which is more than 52 hours per week, more time than they spend in school. If you factor in multitasking with media, this number increases to 10.75 hours per day. These statistics represent an increase in exposure of almost 2.25 hours per day in the last five years (Kaiser Family Foundation Study, 2010). Education needs to appropriately harness this high level of engagement and accessibility or we miss out on a powerful opportunity and tool for learning.

## THE NATIONAL EDUCATION TECHNOLOGY PLAN

The National Education Technology Plan, *Transforming American Education: Learning Powered by Technology,* created by the U.S. Department of Education's Office of Educational Technology (2010) and adopted March 5, 2010, proposes applying the advanced technologies used in our daily personal and professional lives to our nation's education system to improve student learning, accelerate and scale up the implementation of effective instructional practices, and collect and use data for continuous quality improvement. The plan establishes goals and presents recommendations and suggested actions for a model of learning informed by research-based practices and powered by technology for states, districts, the federal government, and other stakeholders to consider.

Building on the thoughts and ideas of a working group of leading researchers and practitioners and on input received from many respected education leaders and the public, this National Education Technology Plan tackles the challenges of integrating technology into all aspects of our educational system. The plan is based on the following assumptions:

- Many of the struggles in our education system stem from our failure to engage the hearts and minds of students.
- What students need to learn and what we know about how they learn have changed, and therefore the learning experiences we provide should change.
- How we assess learning focuses too much on what has been learned after the fact and not enough on improving learning in the moment.
- We miss a huge opportunity to improve our entire education system when we gather student-learning data in silos and fail to integrate the information and make it broadly available to decision makers at all levels of our education system: individual educators, schools, districts, states, and the federal government.
- Learning depends on effective teaching, and we need to focus on extended teams of connected educators with different roles who collaborate within schools and across time and distance, and who use technology resources and tools to augment human talent.
- Effective teaching is an outcome of preparing and continually training teachers and leaders to guide the type of learning we want in our schools.
- Making engaging learning experiences and resources available to all learners anytime and anywhere requires state-of-the-art infrastructures, which include technology, people, and processes that ensure continuous access.
- Education can learn much from such industries as business and entertainment about leveraging technology to continuously improve learning outcomes while increasing the productivity of our education system at all levels.
- Just as in health, energy, and defense, the federal government has an important role to play in funding and coordinating some of the R&D challenges associated with leveraging technology to ensure the maximum opportunity to learn.

In an attempt to support each of these assumptions, the proposed goals address five essential components of learning powered by technology:

Goal 1: Learning

All learners will have engaging and empowering learning experiences both in and out of school that prepare them to be active, creative, knowledgeable, and ethical participants in our globally networked society.

Goal 2: Assessment

Our education system at all levels will leverage the power of technology to measure what matters and use assessment data for continuous improvement.

Goal 3: Teaching

Professional educators will be supported individually and in teams by technology that connects them to data, content, resources, expertise, and learning experiences that can empower and inspire them to provide more effective teaching for all learners.

Goal 4: Infrastructure

All students and educators will have access to a comprehensive infrastructure for learning, when and where they need it.

Goal Five: Productivity

Our education system at all levels will redesign processes and structures to take advantage of the power of technology to improve learning outcomes while making more efficient use of time, money, and staff.

*(U.S. Department of Education Office of Educational Technology, 2010)*

This plan certainly has clear implications for the CCSS initiative. In addition to the goals listed in the 87-page report, there are comprehensive and very specific recommendations that support the implementation of the technology model that has a direct positive relationship to the success of CCSS. The suggestions are too lengthy to cite here, but I encourage all of you who have an interest in or responsibility for this area of educational system reform to become familiar with its contents. It highlights many feasible and realistic considerations for using technology in the service of improved learning for all of our students.

The plan also acknowledges that with the right technology, educators can provide engaging and powerful learning content, resources, and experiences as well as assessment systems that measure student learning in more complete, authentic, and meaningful ways. With technology-based learning and next-generation assessment systems, we can improve student learning and collect data that can be used to continuously develop our entire educational system at all levels. With technology, we can execute collaborative teaching approaches partnered with professional learning strategies that better prepare and enhance educators' competencies and expertise over the course of their careers. With technology, we can redesign and refocus processes to produce better student outcomes while achieving higher levels of productivity and efficiency across the total education system.

As I read through both the executive summary and the plan itself, three things came to mind. First, it is similar to any educational document full of lofty goals that are much easier to discuss than they are to deliver. Still, the recommendations deserve our most diligent and committed efforts to investigate them and the potential for implementing them in conjunction with CCSS. Second, many of the policies and procedures of schools to restrict student access to new digital technologies should be reconsidered. This rethinking of student engagement with social networking tools and other forms of communications inherent in our mobile electronic age should not focus on prohibiting or inhibiting but capitalizing on this accessibility and enthusiasm for digital tools to help meet the education goals, needs, and interests of young people. Finally, all these tools should be expanded in ways that allow educators to have the resources, platforms, and networks to support their professional confidence and competence in incorporating these tools effectively into their classrooms.

## HORIZON REPORT: 2011 K–12 EDITION

The *NMC Horizon Report: 2011 K–12 Edition* (Johnson, Adams, & Haywood, 2011) "examines emerging technologies for their potential impact on and use in teaching, learning, and creative inquiry" in the K–12 educational system. It provides educators with a global perspective about technological issues and trends that are prevalent internationally and offers potential solutions for those challenges. It is the third in a series that introduces six new technologies or practices that will likely enter the mainstream of our educational system within the next one to five years.

Members of the Horizon Project Advisory Board, which is composed mostly of university researchers and corporations, were asked the following questions to consider for inclusion in the report:

- Which of these key technologies will be most important to teaching, learning, or creative expression within the next five years?
- What key technologies are missing from the list?
- What trends do you expect to have a significant impact on the ways in which learning-focused institutions approach our core missions of teaching, research, and service?
- What do you see as the key challenge(s) related to teaching, learning, or creative expression that learning-focused institutions would face during the next five years?

The following made the final list of Emerging Trends, Critical Challenges, and Technologies to Watch.

## Emerging Trends

1. The abundance of resources and relationships made easily accessible via the Internet is increasingly challenging us to revisit our roles as educators in sense-making, coaching, and credentialing.

2. People expect to be able to work, learn, and study whenever and wherever they want.

3. The world of work is increasingly collaborative, giving rise to reflection about the way students' learning projects and performance tasks are structured.

4. The technologies we use are increasingly cloud-based, and our notions of IT support are decentralized.

## Critical Challenges

1. Digital media literacy continues its rise in importance as a key skill in every discipline and profession.

2. Appropriate metrics of evaluation lag behind the emergence of new scholarly forms of authoring, publishing, and researching.

3. Economic pressures and new prototypes of education are presenting unprecedented competition to traditional models of schooling.

4. Keeping pace with the rapid proliferation of information, software tools, and devices is challenging for students and teachers alike.

## Technologies to Watch

1. Electronic Books: Electronic textbooks, online textbooks (Time to Adoption Horizon: One Year or Less)

2. Mobiles: Any computing device you can carry with you and that is easily transportable, such as smartphones, iPads, tablet computers (Time to Adoption Horizon: One Year or Less)

3. Augmented Reality: Adding a computer-assisted layer of contextual information over the real world (Time to Adoption Horizon: Two to Three Years)

4. Game-Based Learning: Using computer games to teach and enhance the curriculum (Time to Adoption Horizon: Two to Three Years)

5. Gesture-Based Computing: Using gestures to interact with the computer (Time to Adoption Horizon: Four to Five Years)

6. Learning Analytics: Using data mining, interpretation, and modeling to improve teaching and learning (Time to Adoption Horizon: Four to Five Years)

Each topic is introduced with an overview that describes what the technology innovation is and how it relates to the improvement of teaching, learning, or creativity. The report includes an annotated list of helpful references for additional study. I encourage a comprehensive review of this report for excellent information and advice to make solid decisions and appropriate choices about how to intelligently infuse technology into our schools and educational system.

## TECHNOLOGICAL IMPLICATIONS FOR CURRICULUM, INSTRUCTION, AND ASSESSMENT

Technology has the proven ability to augment what active learners can learn. It can help them access information to generate new insights as well as access people to help them process those new ideas. In a vibrant learning culture, one in which students and adults are responsible for their own learning and are challenging one another to think deeply about content, well-planned and well-implemented technology enhances everyone's experience. The opportunities are limitless, borderless, and instantaneous. The learning is engaging, relevant, and personalized because it mirrors real work and real life.

Our students were born into a culture and lifestyle where technological immersion and integration is the norm. Our educators are typically the "digital immigrants" who need to adapt and learn how to integrate technology into their personal and professional lives. There is a distinct divide between technology in schools and technology everywhere else, and we need to do something to quickly yet thoughtfully bridge that gap.

An excellent resource to help us with this endeavor is Marc Prensky's book, *Teaching Digital Natives: Partnering for Real Learning* (2010). This book entices me to find a classroom of students somewhere and just dive right into the wonderful world of schools that I miss so much. He describes a "pedagogy of partnering" that honors and addresses the unique needs of 21st century learners. It includes delineating what students are responsible for:

- Finding and following their passion
- Using whatever technology is available
- Researching and finding information
- Answering questions and sharing their thoughts and opinions
- Practicing when properly motivated
- Creating presentations in text and multimedia

And what teachers are responsible for:

- Creating and asking the right questions
- Giving students guidance
- Putting material in context
- Explaining one-on-one
- Creating rigor
- Ensuring quality

Prensky (2010) separates the verbs of learning from the nouns or tools and delineates effective instructional strategies that should exist in a partnering classroom. He emphasizes how important it is to connect essential questions with the big ideas and concepts that are the established learning standards and to choose real problems that need solving to demonstrate deep understanding of standards-based content and skills. His description of a reorganized and restructured learning environment fits "hand-in-glove" with the proposed curriculum, instruction, and assessment focus of CCSS.

The last decade has seen the emergence of some radically redesigned schools, demonstrating the range of possibilities for reforming our current education system. Some are very successful, and we should be looking closer at what is different about them. The ones that are flourishing include schools that organize around demonstrated competence rather than seat time and that enable more flexibility in scheduling and grouping to addresses students' individual learning needs rather than traditional academic periods and lockstep curriculum pacing. Implications for traditional grading systems are also explored in these progressive districts and schools. These schools and classrooms are beginning to incorporate online and digital learning, which offers the opportunity to extend the learning day, week, or year and track performance to measure learning growth, not just achievement.

The United States has a long way to go if we are to see every student complete the College and Career Ready mission to complete at least a year of higher education or postsecondary career training after high school. There is no way to achieve this target until we dramatically reduce the number of students who leave high school without receiving a diploma, which represents half of the enrollment in many urban systems, by the way, or who are unprepared for postsecondary education even if they do graduate. The CCSS initiative is created to support this ambitious goal with designated K–12 benchmarked learning progressions that spiral along the trajectory of high school graduation and to identify students who are at risk for not meeting these learning targets.

A complex set of personal and academic factors underlies students' decisions to leave school or to disengage from learning before graduation, and support should start before children enter kindergarten and become intensified for those students who demonstrate a need for intervention as they move through school. The practices enhanced by the technology that Prensky lists can help address the problem, including learning dashboards that keep students on track with their course requirements and earning credits for courses or entire programs that are completed online.

Redesigning education in America for improved productivity is a complex challenge that will require all CCSS-adopting states representing thousands of districts and schools across the country, the federal government, and other education stakeholders in the public and private sector to collaborate to create and implement innovative solutions. It is an imperative for everyone committed to improving the quality of the learning experience to come together and lead the effort. Technologists must be a part of this conversation.

## MEASURING WHAT MATTERS

This model of learning that Prensky (2010) endorses requires new and better ways to measure what matters in education, to diagnose strengths and weaknesses during the learning process when there is still time to impact and improve student performance—what was referred to as common formative assessments in Chapter 7. Technology-based assessments can provide data to drive decisions on the basis of what is best for every individual student and that, in aggregate, will lead to continuous improvement across our entire education system. Online assessments that combine cognitive research and theory about how students think with the available multimedia, interactivity, and connectivity make it possible to directly assess student acquisition of the verbs that Prensky mentions in his book with the help of the 132 nouns that he lists as possible measurement tools.

When integrated with dynamic learning systems, technology-based assessments can be used formatively to diagnose and modify the conditions of learning and instructional practices and at the same time determine what students have learned for grading and accountability purposes. Furthermore, systems can be designed to capture students' inputs and collect evidence of their knowledge level and problem-solving abilities as they work. Over time, the system "learns" more about students' abilities and can recommend increasingly appropriate interventions. Both assessment consortia, PARCC and SBAC, are investigating this technological capability. With assessments in place that address the full range of expertise and competencies reflected in CCSS standards, student performance data could be collected and analyzed to continually improve learning outcomes and productivity. For example, such data could be used to create a system of interconnected feedback for students, educators, parents, school leaders, and district administrators. For this to work, relevant information must be made available to the right people, at the right time, and in the right format. Educators and leaders at all levels of our system also must be provided with the tools and the training that can help them manage the assessment process, analyze relevant data, and take appropriate action based upon those results.

An important and useful type of assessment that should be included in our conversation about the CCSS learning progressions for English language arts and mathematics is the ipsative assessment, which measures ongoing individual progress toward a goal that highlights and records a student exceeding a personal best. In a climate of getting better at measuring getting better, this concept should be explored and considered a valuable element in the design of next-generation assessment systems. Technology tools are an excellent means of collecting this type of information for students to self-monitor their progress toward meeting a standard.

## TECHNOLOGICAL INFRASTRUCTURES

An infrastructure for learning is always on, always available to students, educators, and parents regardless of their location or time of day. It supports not only access to information, but also access to people and opportunities to participate in online learning communities. It offers a platform on which technologists can build and customize useful applications. An infrastructure for learning unleashes new ways of capturing and sharing knowledge based on the capability of digital media to assimilate text, still and moving images, audio, and other applications that are currently available on a variety of devices. It enables seamless integration of learning both inside and outside of school. It frees learning from a rigid and inflexible transfer model and promotes a much more engaging and personalized learning environment.

On a more operational and practical level, the two assessment consortia, SBAC and PARCC, recommend a technological infrastructure that connects and permits access to data from multiple sources while ensuring appropriate levels of security and privacy necessary on an open system. The platform integrates computer hardware, data and open-source networks, information resources, interoperable software, middleware services, tools, and devices. It supports interdisciplinary teams of professionals responsible for its maintenance and management and for its capacity to potentially transform teaching and learning.

Being configurable for various assessment purposes, the new assessment system should allow for summative, interim, end-of-course, through-course, and adaptive and formative tests and have the capacity to be administered on the same platform.

Imagine this: In the near future, a teacher should be able to utilize the platform to select assessment instruments or items to be used to measure the progress toward a specific benchmark, administer the customized assessment, have it scored, receive a comprehensive report of results that will inform instructional decisions, and finally access curriculum resources and materials that support next steps in the learning sequence. How can we ignore this potential?

Technology exists right now to develop items that allow students to run simulations, engage with real-life scenarios, create graphics, and even play learning-based games. These items can then be scored by the computer in real time and provide additional information to teachers to explain a student's thinking as the question is posed and answered. The use of sophisticated test items that require constructed responses, selected responses, and even performance tasks and events will be feasible with this system. And all of these advantages should be available for less cost, more speed and accessibility, and better quality than exists currently because of the economy of scale offered by the two consortia of states. Again, how can we ignore this potential?

## FROM COMMON SENSE TO COMMON PRACTICE IN TECHNOLOGY

Advances in technology have changed virtually every aspect of our lives. These changes have dramatically impacted how we communicate, manage information, use our time, and complete simple and complex daily tasks. Technology is also reforming how information is discovered and processed. Students are able to access and collect information and interact with others in ways barely thought possible just a few years ago. Electronically, they can visit museums in other countries, participate in lessons taught by teachers conducting research about a relevant topic, engage with scientists in space and under the ocean, view original historic documents, and participate firsthand in limitless learning opportunities with peers across town, across the country, or around the world. Every day, new applications for technology emerge, enhancing both our lives and our learning.

Not only do advances in technology influence how teaching and learning occur for students, they also influence how adults learn. Teachers and principals have opportunities, in virtual classrooms, to participate in multiple professional and personal learning experiences. Teachers can exchange ideas with leading experts in their content areas, visit classrooms of exemplary teachers, receive coaching from their mentors via Web conferencing, and access online resource libraries full of instructional materials and research. Teacher and principal licensure and advanced certificate programs are currently available online nationally and at state universities. Most institutes of higher education offer some online courses, and many now offer entire degree programs online.

The assessment consortia will assume a key role in the transformation of education as well as in their member states, deliberately linking and integrating curriculum, instruction, and assessment for the benefit of students. Measuring student progress both formatively and summatively through the use of technology will improve individual performance and collectively improve the educational system as a whole. Successful implementation of CCSS will rely heavily on the capacity of technology to support this reform initiative.

What this all translates to is what it means to be an effective 21st century teacher, comfortable with the implications that technology will have on a progressive classroom learning environment that needs to be responsive to a new generation of students. To meet these challenges, to successfully implement CCSS, and to be prepared to accept the next generation of assessments, we will need to

- Facilitate, guide, and inspire robust student learning and creativity so that all students have the opportunity to become college and career ready to achieve in a global society
- Support students to maximize the potential of both their formal and informal learning experiences
- Be sensitive to multiple learning modalities when creating differentiated learning experiences for students
- Work as a contributing member of a professional learning community
- Be aware of and utilize the full range of digital tools to enhance student engagement and motivation to improve academic achievement
- Work with students to personalize new learning opportunities and partner with them to create them
- Use data to support student learning and program improvements
- Be lifelong learners
- Be global educators
- Collaborate with policy makers for coherence and change (Resta & Carroll, 2010)

## DO THIS NOW, DO THIS NEXT, AND DO THIS LATER

### Now . . .

Establish a project team that includes technology, library, administrative, and teaching staff to begin brainstorming how to create contemporary digitally compatible learning environments that support the implementation of CCSS.

Begin to prioritize the list of technological needs and wants of your district or school and determine a feasible budget allocation to purchase the essential tools or infrastructure to extend the technological presence in instruction and data management.

Offer some selected professional learning opportunities to the "digital immigrants" so their competence and confidence level of integrating technology into instruction is expanded.

### Next . . .

Read the 2010 National Education Technology Plan (U.S. Department of Education Office of Educational Technology, 2010) and conduct a professional study on topics of interest that are included in the report.

Encourage teachers to use the wiki to share successful lesson plans that address CCSS and begin to build an inventory of well-crafted instructional strategies and activities.

Explore some of the websites listed in the reference section of this book to expand the knowledge base of teachers through professional dialogues.

### Later . . .

Explore what your state is doing to build or extend data management systems that measure student growth and success and provide the necessary information for educators to improve their instructional practices and decisions.

Explore websites such as the Learning Registry (http://www.learning registry.org/), which is a federal project to make learning resources that are managed by the government available to educators.

Commit to researching one website or one webinar a week from the 264 million that are listed when *digital learning* is "googled" and share the information with a teammate or colleague.

## KEY IDEAS FOR CHAPTER 8

→ We must embrace the fact that integrative technology is and will continue to be a significant driver of the education reform movement.

→ We must respond to and support the "digital natives" that currently reside in our classrooms to dispel the student belief that relevant and real learning occurs only outside of the traditional school walls.

→ Comprehensive plans already exist that support the capability of technological infrastructures to more efficiently and effectively educate America's students.

→ The Common Core State Standards incorporate 21st century teaching and learning considerations into their design.

→ The advances of technology will significantly impact curriculum, instruction, and assessment in the next five years.

## QUESTIONS TO CONTINUE THIS DISCUSSION

- ☑ Has the National Educational Technology Plan (NETP) informed or been cited by leaders in your school district as you formulate learning goals as well as strategic plans to meet them?
- ☑ How do you think school leaders should use the NETP goals to reshape and focus our actions as well as current thinking about the role educational technologies play in supporting learning for all students?
- ☑ What does it mean to be digitally literate in an age of constantly evolving technology and resources?
- ☑ How do we capitalize on using these technologies in a productive, creative, and responsible way with our students?
- ☑ What will teaching, learning, and creative expression in schools and classrooms need to look like for educators to adopt emerging technologies to transition from "pockets of innovation" to a "culture of innovation?"

# Accountability for Excellence and Equity

*To be persuasive, we must be believable;*
*To be believable, we must be credible;*
*To be credible, we must be truthful.*

—Edward R. Murrow

Educational accountability is probably one of the most frenetic, feared, and frustrating terms in our current professional language. It typically appears at the center of a heated discussion of extremes, wrought with deep emotion, and represents an all or nothing proposition. The argument might go something like this: "All testing is good; no, all testing is bad. All high-stakes tests are reliable and valid; no, all high-stakes tests are meaningless. All testing results should be considered in making critical educational decisions; no, all results should be discarded and ignored. All systems are innocent victims of the potential gaming of accountability; no, all systems are corrupt and misrepresent results of student performance." And so it goes, this endless debate and tension about the value of our accountability systems, as they are defined and exist today. We can agree that in its current state the system is flawed, but we must reach consensus about how the obligation of accountability for learning, which will remain a vital element in any comprehensive school reform, can become more shared, more internal, more reciprocal, and more holistic.

## UNDERSTANDING TOTAL QUALITY

My experience as an educator during the onset of the accountability era was with the theories of Continuous Quality Improvement (CQI) or Total

Quality Management (TQM) that were being explored by my district at the time. I'll admit I pouted frequently that if I ever saw another PDSA cycle or strategic and operational flowchart again, it would be way too soon. But as with so many unforeseen life events, the study of quality propelled me into a sustained examination of how to deliberately plan for improvement in teaching, learning, and leadership, and that has been my professional mission ever since. And, as a result of this extensive reading and reflection, I now can see clearly distinctive and helpful parallels in our current endeavors for educational excellence and equity with the Common Core State Standards initiative and with the strategies that the quality movement employed.

The suggestions that W. Edwards Deming (in Bonstingl, 1992) offered just after World War II to help Japan rebuild its economy align closely with our attempts to reestablish our faltering educational system. For example, consider these assumptions about quality management:

- We focus on our customers' needs and provide service that at least meets their expectations and oftentimes exceeds them.
- If we are not improving, we are deteriorating or remaining stagnant, and both options are unacceptable in achieving our ultimate goal of measurable improvement in results.
- It is necessary to initiate a team approach, one in which there are vested and empowered partners with the authority to take action in the process of improvement.
- Effective leadership is necessary to break down the barriers and impediments to growth and demonstrate the individual and personal responsibility for change.
- There must be embedded professional development that guides the unified and focused efforts of improvement.
- A deliberate plan for evaluating both the inputs and outcomes of the service is a large part of the improvement process to assess and monitor progress.

My brief list of considerations is relevant to our work as we thoughtfully explore how to move forward with all the parts and pieces of implementing the CCSS initiative and deliberately connect the responsibility of accountability to the entire endeavor.

What do I mean by an improvement system that focuses on enhanced quality such as the proposed CCSS work implies? For me, it is a blueprint or framework for leading an organization to achieve the goals it has established as the priorities for the system. I know from experience that developing an educational improvement plan is very challenging work. It requires clarifying the organizational purpose, defining who the customers are and focusing on them and their needs, identifying and tracking the critical organizational processes that guide the work, developing and analyzing key performance indicators and metrics to measure and monitor progress, benchmarking internal and external research-based practices, using appropriate tools for process improvement, and managing and reporting the data that accurately documents and communicates the results. Bottom line, it is the improvement or accountability system that provides us with the mechanisms for utilizing data to measure and provide evidence of our effectiveness. It is essential in any systemic change effort.

## THE STORY BEHIND THE NUMBERS

Douglas Reeves and my colleagues at the Leadership and Learning Center have generated extensive research and ensuing intellectual property on the important subject of "holistic" or "student-centered" accountability. Our definition represents a philosophically different attitude toward the traditional view of accountability and encourages educators to move past just the numbers indicated in achievement test score averages and include relevant data about curriculum, teaching behaviors, and leadership practices to offer a more complete picture of the relevant influences on student performance. Linda Darling-Hammond refers to this same concept as "genuine" accountability (Darling Hammond, 2006), and I believe it is this distinction that will support the inherent accountability demands of Common Core State Standards.

When we acknowledge and honor the contextual considerations, the story behind the numbers in schools (e.g., student demographics, attendance rates, mobility factors, special student cohorts, teacher qualifications), we are adding a valuable narrative dimension or qualitative explanation that expands the meaning and significance of the typical statistical mean of achievement scores. With further analysis, this enhanced data can help us determine and focus on results that are encouraging and results that are concerning. This more elaborate assessment lens can show the progress of individual students and recognizes that the complexity of what teachers do every day in the classroom cannot be reduced to a single number.

Teachers understand that the ultimate purpose of assessment is improvement in the teaching and learning process. We test to know how to teach more effectively so that our students learn more effectively. It sounds so simplistic, but important ideas usually are. When state testing data are combined with school and classroom information, it can tell us in which areas we are improving and which areas need more attention. This "story" indicates what specific teaching and leadership practices are working with our students so that those adult behaviors become more intentional and can be replicated. Wouldn't this expanded information be less biased and more accurate, less destructive and more constructive, and most important, less confrontational and more compelling? My experience in schools tells me it is worth the additional time and effort to create an accountability picture with data that tells the complete story of a school or district.

## STANDARDS-BASED ACCOUNTABILITY

Since 1990, America has embraced the strategy of standards-based accountability as the systemic reform necessary to fix our failing schools and raise student achievement. In the 1990s, states rushed to develop standardized tests to measure student progress. Public education expenditures doubled. An education summit set lofty goals to be met by 2000. Sadly, none of the goals ever came close to being accomplished in either decade. The same fate looms for the 2014 deadline of NCLB's goal of 100% proficiency in basic skills for all students in America. It is clear that the present system of "accounting" for results is flawed.

Historically, the push for accountability has grown out of a common perception that states initially and traditionally monitored the "inputs" in public education, such as the number of books in the school media center or the number of computers in the lab, but paid little attention to student performance results or the "outputs" of public education. Now that we are competing on a global stage, our audience has extended and become much more sophisticated in what it expects to see as proof of performance, and we have responded by concentrating almost exclusively on student test scores as a measurement of these outputs. Accountability that is actionable and meaningful must find a balance between exploring the causes, the inputs of the system, and the effects or outcomes that we see as a result of our priorities and decisions.

The standards and accountability movement is broadly based politically and remains persistently in the landscape of school reform. It involves elected officials, advocacy groups, professional organizations, and community members who want to accurately measure effectiveness in teaching and learning. The concept emanates from the basic belief that schools, like other public systems in our society, should be able to demonstrate how they contribute to the goals of the organization and that they are responsible for engaging in steady improvement over time. The hope is that increased accountability will promote increased legitimacy and support for public education. This requires a deliberate effort to assess the quality of the educational experience for every student. This is all good, and we should welcome the opportunity to provide valid and reliable evidence of our hard work with students.

## Goals

An accountability system typically begins with a set of goals about what is to be accomplished, or in other words, the desired outcomes of the organization. These goals have a distinct role, because precise standards and measurement tools emanate from them. They should be SMART: specific, measureable, achievable, realistic, and timely. The Common Core State Standards explicitly state their goal is to ensure that all of our students are college and career ready at the end of high school and are prepared to successfully compete in a global economy.

## Standards

Standards present the details of what is expected. As with CCSS, they create boundaries or domains for focus, study, and measurement. Anchor standards delineate the extent to which students are expected to demonstrate mastery of a prioritized body of content and skills that has been designated by an authoritative group of experts as representative of a proficient and acceptable knowledge base. In our case, this offers an extension of the prior initiative led by the CCSSO and NGA to develop College and Career Readiness (CCR) standards in reading, writing, speaking, listening, and language, as well as in mathematics.

The CCR standards, as the backbone for the present Common Core State Standards documents, provide the framework on which to build grade-specific K–12 standards to translate the broad aims of the CCR standards into learning progressions that designate age-appropriate expectations for CCSS. As a result, the CCSS profess to be fewer, clearer, and higher than what currently exists in individual state standards. And many organizations, such as the Thomas B. Fordham Institute, acknowledge and endorse that CCSS has done just that: The new standards are more concise, more specific, and much more rigorous than most state standards that exist today.

## Measurement

The most controversial issue about statewide accountability systems involves the tools and means used to determine compliance with the mandates of the standards. Proving that the standards have been met requires some sort of valid and reliable measurement. This in turn mandates several decisions about who to measure; what approaches to use; how to create useful metrics; and, frequently, where to set the cut-scores for evidence in meeting the standards. Typically this is where the accountability discussion gets messy.

The two consortia responsible for designing these assessment systems are thoughtfully competent in considering all of the elements in a quality assessment framework. Both PARCC and SBAC are acutely aware of the challenge they have accepted to accurately assess the new standards and provide useful information about not only the external accountability expectations, but also the internal organizational benefits of knowing student performance levels and the effective teaching and leadership practices that contribute to improved achievement. We are in good hands with the experts who have agreed to develop a model of accountability that will accelerate our improvement efforts by providing timely, useful, and comprehensive data about student progress in meeting CCSS. These measurements will indicate where we start on our school improvement journey and point us in the direction of a common destination for the first time in our country's history.

## Reporting

Report cards or communication protocols for schools are typically prepared and published to inform both internal and external stakeholders about the progress made toward the achievement of stated goals. Sometimes ratings or rank order comparisons are included, and therein lies a great deal of the controversy about how the accountability function of high-stakes tests actually documents student progress. The difficulty with most of these reports is the lack of computational transparency and consistency that can potentially lead to problems when serious negative consequences are attached to measured low performance. The NCLB dilemma is a case in point. The solution is a more comprehensive framework of accountability that has the potential to tell the whole story of each school's efforts to provide educational excellence and equity to all of its students.

The Leadership and Learning Center recommends five key components in effective accountability systems that are communicated frequently and consistently. The purpose of the accountability report is to provide data to assess the level of accomplishment of the stated goals and make informed decisions about planning next steps based upon that information. These five elements of holistic accountability are systemwide indicators, school-based indicators, information about the demographics of the student population, qualitative descriptions of the unique school environments, and how the results are to be used to determine effective practices that will promote improved teaching and learning. When all of these factors are connected and considered, the potential for growth and development of our work is enhanced immeasurably.

## Connecting the Accountability Dots

In addition to recommending the five indicators that extend the usefulness and importance of a comprehensive accountability system to support improvement, there are six principles recommended by the Leadership and Learning Center that represent the determining factors in a quality accountability system:

- Congruence between the recognized and rewarded goals of the organization and the alignment and consistency of adult actions in meeting those goals
- Specificity and clarity of the action plan designed to communicate the "who, what, why, how, and how well" of the strategies designed to support effective implementation of the plan
- Respect for diversity of ideas and opinions from both students and adults to help represent a broader perspective and align the goals of the system to benefit everyone
- Continuous improvement efforts that are focused, sustained, and based upon data
- Universality of responsibility to reinforce the value of open and transparent communication about where students are relative to where they need to be and how everyone in the system will work together to close that gap
- Reciprocity of building the capacity to do the work and listening to and solving the issues that impede progress

The combination of the critical five indicators that tell the complete story of accountability and the six principles of quality can begin a very robust, comprehensive, and indeed, necessary dialogue about the direction improvement efforts take in each school and district in our nation. It is a vital step in the thorough and thoughtful implementation of CCSS.

## TEACHERS TAKE THE LEAD

I recommend that teachers use their capacity for understanding good instructional practices in their own contexts to move the accountability movement ahead much further and faster than what external auditing has the potential of doing. We should stop being told what to do and initiate and highlight our own measures of success. If teachers engage in collaborative self-study and courageous conversations to determine what effective teaching and learning looks like and how they can individually and collectively contribute to improved student achievement, they participate in what Richard Elmore calls "internal accountability" (2002, p. 20). Schools where this takes place have a strong "internal" focus on instruction and clear expectations for teacher, leader, and student performance.

The only way out of this current accountability dilemma is to recognize that we are our own best advocates. Only by telling our story, by providing qualitative and quantitative information on the enormous amount of work that occurs in the classroom, can we begin to balance the scales of cause and effect data, and bring some sense and logic to educational accountability. Only by providing relevant and authentic reflection on the benefits of a common curriculum and aligned teaching practices can we provide context to the box scores that now dominate the traditional field of accountability and the limiting and incomplete measures of results.

Teachers need to tell their professional story comprehensively and persuasively about the daily and detailed work they do, without excuses and without apology. When colleagues build their capacity to reach consensus about what constitutes a high-quality education for all of our students based upon rigorous standards of performance, we can then work on the specific problems that impede our progress. We can develop new adult knowledge and skills that will support success, and celebrate the improved results in student achievement that will emanate from this universal goal.

## SYSTEM THINGS: NOT SINGLE THINGS

An incredibly informative and comprehensive education report, *How the World's Most Improved School Systems Keep Getting Better* (Mourshed, Chijioke, & Barber, 2010), was issued in November 2010 as a follow-up to the 2007 publication, *How the World's Best Performing School Systems Come Out on Top* published by McKinsey and Company. In it is a detailed description of 20 educational systems from around the world, all with improving but differing levels of performance, that have experienced significant, sustained, and widespread gains in student outcomes as measured by international and national assessments. This report addresses the research question of which aspects of school system reform interventions are universal and which are context specific. Almost every nation in the world has introduced some sort of reform effort during the past two decades, but very few have succeeded in moving their systems from poor to fair, fair to good, good to great, and great to excellent.

In this extensive analysis, the authors discovered a small number of critical factors that collectively create the synergy necessary for pervasive improvement. Each of these common attributes represents clusters of interventions that identify transferable reform elements for school systems, no matter what their starting point. Based on more than 200 interviews with system stakeholders and examination of some 600 interventions carried out by these systems, this report identifies the reform elements that are replicable for school systems everywhere as they move from poor to fair, to good, to great, to excellent performance.

The systems that were studied were Armenia; Aspire (a U.S. charter school system); Boston, Massachusetts; Chile; England; Ghana; Hong Kong; Jordan; Latvia Lithuania; Long Beach, California; Madhya Pradesh, India; Minas Gerais, Brazil; Ontario, Canada; Poland; Saxony, Germany; Singapore; Slovenia; South Korea; and Western Cape, South Africa. Valuable lessons and parallels that can inform the work of CCSS are obvious in every aspect of this study.

---

In each case it is very clear that all improving entities, even if their starting point is dismal, are led by a combination of leaders who are self-aware that they are engaged in a phenomenon that the report calls "it's a system thing"—a small number of critical factors that go together to create the chemistry of widespread improvement. We see the clusters of interventions, different for those starting from a weak base than those who have already had significant success. We see the pathways playing themselves out in each type of context. We see what it takes to ignite system change, what specific strategies achieve breakthrough, what interventions build ever-increasing momentum, how systems can sustain improvement, and especially how they can go to the next stage of development. As someone who has worked explicitly on system change in several contexts since 1997, including being directly involved in helping to lead whole system reform in Ontario since 2003, I can say that *How the World's Most Improved School Systems Keep Getting Better* makes a one of a kind seminal contribution to this dynamic and critical field. It couldn't come at a more propitious time. Finally, we are witnessing across the globe a robust anticipatory and proactive interest in OECD's Programme for International Student Achievement (PISA). PISA is no longer just a "results phenomenon." PISA leaders are increasingly getting at what lies behind the numbers and are thus generating key insights and questions. The *How the World's Most Improved School Systems Keep Getting Better* report goes further, much further, in portraying the inner workings of successful pathways of reform given different beginning points.

*(Mourshed, Chijioke, & Barber, 2010)*

Some pervasive and very germane discoveries were made in this study. What we learn from this report can have significant implications for the work we will accomplish in implementing CCSS. For example, each system at each performance level selects a critical mass of appropriate intervention strategies and implements them with fidelity. In a system that is moving from poor to fair, concentration is given to supporting the acquisition of the basic skills of literacy and numeracy for students and the acquisition of basic instructional strategies for the teachers. At the next level of performance, fair to good, systems are reviewing and analyzing accountability data to create organizational structures that maintain continuous student academic growth and enhanced teacher practices. Moving from good to great, systems focus on the development of their people, teachers, and leaders and the career paths that support both the individual's goals and the organizational goals. Last, the great to excellent group works to encourage school-based ownership of innovation and experimentation to improve student and adult performance.

What is noteworthy about this report and offers great potential to the CCSS implementation efforts is that

- Each performance level begins with specific interventions that are appropriate and supportive at that stage of development
- Each intervention is implemented, monitored, and adjusted to meet the varied needs of the system
- Each level indicates a progressive movement from a very centralized accountability system to a site-based one
- Each improving system "prescribes adequacy but unleashes greatness"
- Each system works across all levels to revise curriculum and standards, to ensure a fair compensation structure, to build technical capacity, assess students comprehensively, establish data systems, and introduce policies and procedures that sustain progress (Mourshed, Chijioke, & Barber, 2010)

I encourage my colleagues to review this extensive report to discover the many commonalities that these 20 global systems experienced to guide and direct our work with CCSS.

## FROM COMMON SENSE TO COMMON PRACTICE IN HOLISTIC ACCOUNTABILITY

Well, that is my brief take on the often "testy" subject of accountability. I have learned through years of experience that accountability systems don't cause schools to improve; they create the conditions in which it is advantageous for schools to collaboratively work on specific problems and find solutions. Their purpose is to act like the sun and provide a bright light on what is happening in schools and districts to help illuminate what is working so that it continues and clarifies what is not working so that it changes. But just like the sun, accountability implies sometimes seeing the light and sometimes feeling the heat. In recent years, the term has generated much more of the latter response, and we need to work collectively to regain the positive balance of taking responsibility for the authority to act and the resultant effects of assuming that public accountability for the benefit of all of our nation's children.

In summary, I offer a beautiful sentiment that a colleague from the Leadership and Learning Center shared from her recent trip to Zambia. In the very sparsely furnished and equipped facility at the University Teaching Hospital School for Special Needs Students hangs a poster that says it all. Good luck with everything.

Just Try

Try,

Try more.

Try one more time.

Try it a little differently.

Try it again tomorrow.

Try and ask for help.

Try to find someone who has done it before.

Try to determine what is working.

Just keep trying.

—Author unknown

## DO THIS NOW, DO THIS NEXT, AND DO THIS LATER

### Now . . .

#### Collaboratively

Examine your current accountability data and the current accountability report format to determine how effective these communication tools are for the variety of publics this information reaches.

Examine the accountability data to determine the current level of student performance and identify areas of academic strength and need.

Determine if there are multiple indicators of success that highlight academic performance or if there are missing pieces of information that would support relaying the "whole story" of what is happening with students and adults in the system.

## Next . . .

Investigate the elements of a "holistic," "internal," or "genuine" accountability system to ensure they are included in a new or enhanced plan created to support CCSS implementation.

Create visible data walls that provide evidence of student growth and promote dialogue among staff members about the positive adult practices that support this progress.

Collectively spend ample time as a data team or professional learning team to draw inferences from the data that identify effective learning, teaching, and leadership strategies and indicators that can be replicated.

## Later . . .

Expand the data collection process to include post-secondary performance information about students after they leave K–12 education to determine how successful the CCSS have been in preparing them for college and careers.

Widen the communication platform to include all stakeholders and hold them accountable for improved student results and an improved education system as well.

Read, read, read some more, and reflect and reflect more deeply about how all of these components of an effective accountability system bring to light the considerations and implications for a quality education experience for America's students and adults.

## KEY IDEAS FOR CHAPTER 9

→ Accountability for learning will remain a vital element in any comprehensive school reform and needs to become more shared, more internal, more reciprocal, and more holistic.

→ The goal of an accountability system is to foster and sustain excellence and equity in educational opportunities for all of our students.

→ We need a balance of information about the "inputs" and "outputs" to measure effectiveness.

→ Effective accountability systems include the story behind the numbers to provide an explanation about how students are performing and, more important, why they are performing as they are and what adult actions will improve their performance.

→ Establishing the Common Core State Standards is an attempt to rationally provide the dimensions of accountability to our educational system.

## QUESTIONS TO CONTINUE THIS DISCUSSION

☑ How do we as educators counter the current myopic and limited view of responsibilities inherent in the demands for accountability?

☑ What are the most challenging and crucial questions that your current accountability data identify?

☑ What are the important and helpful indicators and qualities that an effective and comprehensive accountability system would include?

☑ What information do internal and external stakeholders need to know to fairly evaluate the success of a school or district?

# References

Achieve, Inc. (2010, August). *On the road to implementation: Achieving the promise of the common core state standards.* Retrieved from http://www.achieve.org/achievingcommoncore_implementation

Ainsworth, L. (2010). *Rigorous curriculum design: How to create curriculum units of study that align standards, instruction, and assessment.* Englewood, CO: Lead+Learn Press.

Albert Shanker Institute. (2011). *A call for common content.* Retrieved from http://www.ashankerinst.org/curriculum.html

ASCD. (1997, December). *Conference report: Airing our differences.* Retrieved from http://www.ascd.org/publications/newsletters/education-update/dec97/vol39/num08/Airing-Our-Differences.aspx

Bonstingl, J. (1992, November). "The quality revolution in education." *Educational Leadership (50)* 3, 4–9.

Boyer, E. L. (1995). *The basic school: A community for learning.* San Francisco, CA: Jossey-Bass.

Collins, J. (2001). *Good to great: Why some companies make the leap and others don't.* New York, NY: Harper Collins.

Common Core State Standards Initiative. (2010a, June). *Common Core State Standards for English language arts and literacy in history/social studies/science, and technical subjects.* Retrieved from http://www.corestandards.org/assets/CCSI_ELA%20Standards.pdf

Common Core State Standards Initiative. (2010b, June). *Common Core State Standards for mathematics.* Retrieved from http://www.corestandards.org/assets/CSSI_Mathematics%20Standards.pdf

Common Core State Standards Initiative. (n.d.). *English language arts standards: Introduction—Key design considerations.* Retrieved from http://www.corestandards.org/the-standards/english-language-arts-standards/introduction/key-design-considerations/

Council of Chief State School Officers. (2008). *The interstate school leader's licensure consortium (ISLLC) standards.* Retrieved from http://www.ccsso.org/Resources/Publications/Educational_Leadership_Policy_Standards_ISLLC_2008_as_Adopted_by_the_National_Policy_Board_for_Educational_Administration.html

Council of Chief State School Officers. (2011). *The Interstate Teacher Assessment and Support Consortium (In TASC) Standards.* Retrieved from http://www.ccsso.org/Resources/Programs/Interstate_Teacher_Assessment_Consortium_(InTASC).html

Covey, S. R. (1990). *Principal-centered leadership.* New York, NY: Summit Books.

Danielson, C. (2007). *Enhancing professional practice: A framework for teaching* (2nd ed.). Alexandria, VA: ASCD.

Darling-Hammond, L. (1997). *The right to learn: A blueprint for creating schools that work.* New York, NY: John Wiley and Sons.

Darling-Hammond, L. (2006). *Standards, assessments, and educational policy: In pursuit of genuine accountability.* Princeton, NJ: Educational Testing Service.

Dewey, J. (1917). *Democracy and education.* New York, NY: Macmillan Publishing Company.

Dickens, C. (1859). *A tale of two cities.* New York, NY: Penguin Books.

DuFour, R., DuFour, R., & Eaker, R. (2008). *Revisiting professional learning communities at work: New insights for improving schools.* Bloomington, IN: Solution Tree.

Dweck, C. (2008). *Mindset: The new psychology of success.* New York, NY: Ballentine Press.

Edutopia. (2011). *Classroom guide: Top ten tips for assessing project-based learning.* The George Lucas Educational Foundation. Retrieved from http://www.edutopia.org/node/51840/?download=yes

Elmore, R. E. (2002). *Bridging the gap between standards and achievement: The imperative for professional development in education.* Albert Shanker Institute. Retrieved from http://www.shankerinstitute.org

Fordham Institute. (2010, July). *The state of state standards—and the common core in 2010.* Retrieved from http://www.edexcellence.net/publications-issues/publications/the-state-of-state.html

Frankl, V. E. (2006). *Man's search for meaning.* Boston, MA: Beacon Press.

Fullan, M. (2001). *Leading in a culture of change: Being effective in complex times.* San Francisco, CA: Jossey-Bass.

Fullan, M., Cuttress, C., & Kilcher, A. (2005, Fall). Eight forces for leaders of change. *Journal of Staff Development, 26*(4), 54–58.

Gewertz, C. (2011, April). "Gates, Pearson partner to craft common core curriculum." *Education Week.* Retrieved from http://edweek.org/ew/articles/2011/04/27/30pearson.h30.html

Guskey, T. R. (2000). *Evaluating professional development.* Thousand Oaks, CA: Corwin.

Hansel, L. (Ed.). (2010–2011, Winter). Either it all works together or it hardly works at all: How a common core curriculum could make our education system run like clockwork [Entire issue]. *American Educator, 34*(4).

Hattie, J. A. (2009). *Visible learning: A synthesis of over 800 meta-analyses relating to achievement.* New York, NY: Routledge.

Johnson, L., Adams, S., & Haywood, K. (2011). *The NMC Horizon Report: 2011 K–12 edition.* Austin, TX: The New Media Consortium.

jreeves. (2010, November 17). *2010 Blue Ribbon Schools ceremony celebrates teachers and principals* [Web log post]. Retrieved from http://www.ed.gov/blog/2010/11/2010-blue-ribbon-schools-ceremony-celebrates-teachers-and-principals/

Kaiser Family Foundation Study. (2010). *Generation M2: Media in the lives of 8- to 18-year-olds.* Retrieved from www.kff.org/entmedia/upload/8010.pdf

Learning Forward. (2011). *Standards for professional learning.* Retrieved from http://www.learningforward.org/standards/index.cfm

Littky, D. (2004). *The big picture: Education is everyone's business.* Alexandria, VA: ASCD.

Marzano, R. (1992). *A different kind of classroom: Teaching with dimensions of learning.* Alexandria, VA: ASCD.

Marzano, R. (2009, September). Setting the record straight on "high-yield" strategies. *Phi Delta Kappan, 91*(1), 30–37.

Marzano, R., Pickering, D., & Pollock, J. (2001). *Classroom instruction that works: Research-based strategies for increasing student achievement.* Alexandria, VA: ASCD.

McNulty, B., & Besser, L. (2011). *Leaders make it happen! An administrator's guide to Data Teams.* Englewood, CO: Lead+Learn Press.

McREL. (n.d.). *What is Dimensions of Learning?* Retrieved from http://www.mcrel.org/dimensions/whathow.asp

McTighe, J. (1996/1997). What happens between assessments? *Educational Leadership, 54* (4), 6–12.

Mourshed, M., Chijioke, C., & Barber, M. (2010). "How the world's most improved school systems keep getting better." McKinsey & Company. Retrieved from http://mckinseyonsociety.com/how-the-worlds-most-improved-school-systems-keep-getting-better/

National Association of Elementary School Principals. (2009). *Leading learning communities: Standards for what principals should know and do.* Retrieved from www.naesp.org/resources/1/Pdfs/LLC2-ES.pdf

National Board for Professional Teaching Standards. (2012). *The standards.* Retrieved from http://www.nbpts.org/the_standards

National Commission on Excellence in Education. (1983, April). *A nation at risk: The imperative for educational reform.* Retrieved from http://reagan.procon.org/sourcefiles/a-nation-at-risk-reagan-april-1983.pdf

National Council of Teachers of Mathematics. (2011, January). *Making it happen: A guide to interpreting and implementing Common Core State Standards for mathematics.* Retrieved from http://www.nctm.org/news/content.aspx?id=27819

The New Basics Project. (n.d.a). *The new basics project.* Retrieved from http://education.qld.gov.au/corporate/newbasics

The New Basics Project. (n.d.b). *The rich tasks.* Retrieved from http://education.qld.gov.au/corporate/newbasics/html/richtasks/richtasks.html

Partnership for Assessment of Readiness for College and Careers (PARCC). (2010, June). *The PARCC application for the Race to the Top comprehensive assessment systems competition.* Retrieved from http://www.fldoe.org/parcc/pdf/apprtcasc.pdf

Perkins, D. (1993). *Smart schools.* New York, NY: Simon and Schuster.

Pink, D. (2009). *Drive: The surprising truth about what motivates us.* New York, NY: Riverhead Books.

Popham, W. J. (2008). *Transformative assessment.* Alexandria, VA: ASCD.

Prensky, M. (2010). *Teaching digital natives: Partnering for real learning.* Thousand Oaks, CA: Corwin.

Reeves, D. B. (2002). *Reason to write: Help your child succeed in school and in life through better reasoning and clear communication.* New York, NY: Kaplan Publishing.

Reeves, D. B. (2006). *The learning leader: How to focus school improvement for better results.* Alexandria, VA: ASCD.

Reeves, D. B. (2008). *Reframing teacher leadership to improve your school.* Alexandria, VA: ASCD.

Reeves, D. B. (2010). Standards, assessment, and accountability: Real questions from educators. Englewood, CO: Lead+Learn Press.

Reeves, D. B. (2011). *Finding your leadership focus: What matters most for student results.* New York, NY: Teachers College Press.

Resta, P., & Carroll, T. (2010). *Redefining teacher education for Digital Age learners.* Retrieved from www.redefineteachered.org

Rose, A., Peery, A., Pitchford, B., Doubek, B., Kamm, C., Allison, E., Cordova, J., Nielsen, K., Besser, L., Campsen, L., Gregg, L., White, M., & Ventura, S. (2010). *Data teams: The big picture.* Englewood, CO: Lead + Learn Press.

Schmoker, M. (2006). *Results now: How we can achieve unprecedented improvement in teaching and learning.* Alexandria, VA: ASCD.

Schmoker, M. (2011). *Focus: Elevating the essentials to radically improve student learning.* Alexandria, VA: ASCD.

Senge, P. (1990). *The fifth discipline: The art and practice of the learning organization.* New York, NY: Doubleday.

SMARTER Balanced Assessment Consortium (SBAC). (2010, June). *Race to the Top assessment program application for new grants: Comprehensive assessment systems.* Retrieved from http://www.k12.wa.us/SMARTER/pubdocs/SBAC_Narrative.pdf

Stiggins, R. (2005). *Student-involved assessment for learning* (4th ed.). Upper Saddle River, NJ: Prentice Hall.

Tomlinson, C. A. (1999). *The differentiated classroom: Responding to the needs of all learners.* Alexandria, VA: ASCD.

U.S. Department of Education. (2009). *Race to the Top assessment program.* Retrieved from http://www2.ed.gov/programs/racetothetop-assessment/index.html

U.S. Department of Education, Office of Educational Technology. (2010). *Transforming American education: Learning powered by technology.* National Education Technology Plan. Retrieved from http://www.ed.gov/technology/netp-2010

van Leeuwen, F. (2011, March 16). International Summit on the Teaching Profession, New York, NY. Education International. Retrieved from http://www.ei-ie.org

White, S. (2009). *Leadership maps.* Englewood, CO: Lead+Learn Press.

White, S. (2011a). *Beyond the numbers: Making data work for teachers and school leaders* (2nd ed.). Englewood, CO: Lead+Learn Press.

White, S. (2011b). *Show me the proof: Tools and strategies to make data work with the Common Core State Standards* (2nd ed.). Englewood, CO: Lead+Learn Press.

Wiggins, G. (1998). *Educative assessment.* San Francisco, CA: Jossey-Bass.

Wiggins, G., & McTighe, J. (2005). *Understanding by design* (2nd ed.). Alexandria, VA: ASCD.

Wiliam, D. (2007–2008). Changing classroom practice. *Educational Leadership, 65*(4), 36–42.

# Suggested Reading

Achieve, Inc. (2010, August). *Aligning assessments with the Common Core State Standards.* Retrieved from http://www.achieve.org/files/CCSS&Assessments .pdf

Achieve, Inc. (2011, September). *The future ready project.* Retrieved from http://www.futurereadyproject.org/messaging

ACT. (2006). *Benefits of a high school core curriculum.* Iowa City, IA: Author. Retrieved from http://www.act.org/research/policymakers/pdf/core_cur riculum.pdf

ACT. (2010). *Mind the gaps: How college readiness narrows achievement gaps in college success.* Iowa City, IA: Author. Retrieved from www.act.org/research/ policymakers/pdf/MindTheGaps.pdf

Ainsworth, L., & Viegut, D. (2006). *Common formative assessments: How to connect standards-based instruction and assessment.* Thousand Oaks, CA: Corwin.

Allison, E., et al. (2010). *Data teams: The big picture.* Englewood, CO: Lead+Learn Press.

Almeida, L., et al. (2011). *Standards and assessment: The core of quality instruction.* Englewood, CO: Lead+Learn Press.

*American Educator.* (2011, Spring). [Entire edition]. *35*(1).

Barth, R. S. (2001). *Learning by heart.* San Francisco, CA: Jossey-Bass.

Bryk, A. S., Gomez, L. M., & Grunow, A. (2010). *Getting ideas into action: Building networked improvement communities in education.* Retrieved from http:// www.carnegiefoundation.org/spotlight/webinar-bryk-gomez-building-net worked-improvement-communities-in-education

Center for K–12 Assessment and Performance Assessment (2010, February). *Coming together to raise achievement: New assessments for the common core state standards.* Retrieved from http://www.k12center.org/publications/ assessment_consortia.html

Center on Education Policy. (2011, January). *States' progress and challenges in implementing common core state standards.* Retrieved from http://www.cep-dc .org/cfcontent_file.cfm?

Common Core. (2009). *Why we're behind: What top nations teach their students but we don't.* Washington, DC: Author.

Common Core State Standards Initiative. (2010, June). *Preparing America's students for college & career.* Retrieved from http://www.corestandards.org

Common Core State Standards Initiative. (2010, June 30). *Common Core State Standards webinar.* Retrieved from http://www.corestandards.org

Common Core State Standards Initiative. (n.d.). *Standards-setting considerations.* Retrieved from www.corestandards.org/assets/Considerations.pdf

Conley, D. T. (2011, March). Building on the common core. *Educational Leadership, 68*(6), 16–21.

Danielson, C. (2009). *Talk about teaching! Leading professional conversations.* Thousand Oaks, CA: Corwin.

Darling-Hammond, L. (2000). Teacher quality and student achievement: A review of state policy evidence. *Education Policy Analysis Archives, 8*(1), 1–49.

Darling-Hammond, L. (2010a). *Performance counts: Assessment systems that support high-quality learning.* Washington, DC: Council of Chief State School Officers.

Darling-Hammond, L. (2010b). *The flat world and education: How America's commitment to equity will determine our future.* New York, NY: Teachers College Press.

Darling-Hammond, L., & Pecheone, R. (2010). *Developing an internationally comparable balanced assessment system that supports high-quality learning.* Princeton, NJ: Educational Testing Services.

DuFour, R., DuFour, R., & Elmore, R. E. (2000). *Building a new structure for school leadership.* Albert Shanker Institute. Retrieved from http://www.shankerinstitute.org

Education Commission of the States. (2007). *High school graduation requirements: Foreign language.* Denver, CO: Author.

Education International. (2011, March). *EI general secretary tells summit nations are built on public schools.* Retrieved from http://ei-ie.org/en/news/news_details/1708

Education Northwest. (2011, October). *Spotlight on the common core state standards.* Retrieved from http://educationnorthwest.org/resource/1335

Finn, C. E., & Pertill, M. J. (2010, October). *Now what? Imperatives and options for "common core" implementation and governance.* Retrieved from http://www.edexcellence.net/publications-issues/publications/now-what-imperatives-and.html

Fordham Foundation. (2011). *ESEA briefing book.* Retrieved from http://www.edexcellence.net/publications/esea-briefing-book.html

Foundation for Excellence in Education. (2010). *Digital learning now report.* Retrieved from http://www.digitallearningnow.com/

Fullan, M. (2005). *Leadership and sustainability: System thinkers in action.* Thousand Oaks, CA: Corwin.

Fullan, M. (2008). *The six secrets of change.* Retrieved from www.schoolbriefing.com/1070/six-secrets-of-change-essential-lessons-for-school-leaders/

Fullan, M. (2010). *The moral imperative realized.* Thousand Oaks, CA: Corwin.

Gewertz, C. (2010, June). Final version of core standards assuages some concerns. *Education Week, 33*(9), 18–19.

Gewertz, C. (2011, April 27). Gates, Pearson partner to craft common-core curricula. *Education Week.* Retrieved from http://edweek.org/ew/articles/2011/04/27/30perason.h30.html

Guskey, T. R. (2002). *Professional development and teacher change.* Retrieved from academic.research.microsoft.com/Paper/5985521.aspx?viewType=1

Guskey, T. R. (2003, February). How classroom assessments improve learning. *Educational Leadership, 60*(5), 6–11.

Harvard Graduate School of Education. (2011, February). *Pathways to prosperity: Meeting the challenge of preparing young Americans for the 21st century.* Retrieved from http://www.gse.harvard.edu/news-impact/2011/02/pathways-to-prosperity-meeting-the-challenge-of-preparing-young-americans-for-the-21st-century/

Hawley, W., & Valli, L. (1999). The essentials of effective professional development: A new consensus. In L. Darling-Hammond & G. Sykes (Eds.), *Teaching as the learning profession: Handbook of Policy and Practice.* San Francisco, CA: Jossey-Bass.

Hayes-Jacobs, H. (2010). *Curriculum 21: Essential education for a changing world.* Alexandria, VA: ASCD.

Heritage, M. (2010a). *Formative assessment and next-generation assessment systems: Are we losing an opportunity?* Washington, DC: Council of Chief State School Officers.

Heritage, M. (2010b). *Formative assessment: Making it happen in the classroom.* Thousand Oaks, CA: Corwin.

Holt, T. (2010). *Moving education through technology integration ebook.* Retrieved from http://www.al.atomiclearning.com/lp=26

International Center for Leadership in Education. (2010, August). *Common core state standards initiative: Classroom implications for 2014.* Retrieved from http://www.leadered.com/whitepapers.html

King, J. E. (2011, January). *Implementing the common core state standards: An action agenda for higher education.* American Council on Education. Retrieved from http://www.acenet.edu/links/pdfs/cpa/ImplementingTheCommonCoreStateStandards_2011.html

Marzano, R. (2003). *What works in schools: Translating research into action.* Alexandria, VA: ASCD.

Marzano, R. (2007a). *The art and science of teaching: A comprehensive framework for effective instruction.* Alexandria, VA: ASCD.

Marzano, R. (2007b). *The art and science of teaching.* Alexandria, VA: ASCD.

Marzano, R., Waters, T., & McNulty, B. (2005). *School leadership that works: From research to results.* Alexandria, VA: ASCD.

Mathis, W. (2010, July). *The common core standards initiative: An effective reform tool?* Retrieved from www.nepccolorado.edu/author/mathis-william-j

McTigue, J., Elliott, S., & Wiggins, G. (2004, September) You can teach for meaning. *Educational Leadership, 62*(1), 26–30.

Munson, L. (2011, March). What students need to learn. *Educational Leadership, 68*(6), 10–15.

NGA, CCSSO, & Achieve Inc. (2008). *Benchmarking for success: Ensuring U.S. students receive a world-class education.* Retrieved from http://www.achieve.org/BenchmarkingforSuccess

Nye, B., Konstantopoulos, S., & Hedges, L. (2004). How large are teacher effects? *Educational Evaluation and Policy Analysis, 26*(3), 237–257.

OECD. (2010). *PISA 2009 results: Executive summary.* Retrieved from http://www.mcgraw-hillresearchfoundation.org/mhrf-pisa-paper

OECD. (2011). *Lessons from PISA for the United States: Strong performers and successful reformers in education.* OECD Publishing. Retrieved from http://dx.doi.org/10.1787/9789264096660-en

Pashler, H., et al. (2007). *Organizing instruction and study to improve student learning (NCER 2007–2004)*. Washington, DC: National Center for Education Research, Institute of Education Sciences, U.S. Department of Education. Retrieved from http://ncer.ed.gov

Peery, A. (2009). *Writing matters in every classroom*. Englewood, CO: Lead+Learn Press.

Petrilli, M., & Finn, C. E., Jr. (2011, May 12). Fordham responds to the common core "counter manifesto." *Education Next*. Retrieved from http://education next.org/fordham-responds-to-the-common-core-counter-manifesto/

Programme for International Student Assessment. (2009). *In what students know and can do: Student performance in reading, mathematics and science*. Paris: Organisation for Economic Cooperation and Development. Retrieved from www.pisa.oecd.org/dataoecd/54/12/46643496.pdf

Quillen, I. (2011). *E-learning update: Report shows blended examples*. Retrieved from http://blogs.edweek.org/edweek/DigitalEducation/2011/05/elearn ing_update_study_shows_b.html

Ravitch, D. (2010). *The death and life of the great American school system: How testing and choice are undermining education*. Philadelphia, PA: Basic Books.

Reeves, D. B. (2000). *Accountability in action: A blueprint for learning organizations*. Englewood, CO: Advanced Learning Centers, Inc.

Reeves, D. B. (2002a). *The leader's guide to standards: A blueprint for educational equity and excellence*. San Francisco, CA: Jossey-Bass.

Reeves, D. B. (2002b). *Holistic accountability: Serving students, schools, and community*. Thousand Oaks, CA: Corwin.

Reeves, D. B. (2004). *Accountability for learning: How teachers and school leaders can take charge*. Alexandria, VA: ASCD.

Reeves, D. B. (2009). *Leading change in your school: How to conquer myths, build commitment, and get results*. Alexandria, VA: ASCD.

Reeves, D. B. (2010a). Getting ready for national standards. *ASCD Express*, 5(8).

Reeves, D. B. (2010b). *Transforming professional development into student results*. Alexandria, VA: ASCD.

Senechal, D. (2010, Spring). The most daring education reform of all. *American Educator, 34*(1), 4–16.

Sloan, W. (2010). Coming to terms with common core standards. *ASCD Info Brief, 16*(4).

Speck, M., & Knipe, C. (2005). *Why can't we get it right? Designing high quality professional development for standards-based schools*. Thousand Oaks, CA: Corwin.

Stiggins, R. (2006). *Balanced assessment systems: Redefining excellence in assessment*. Princeton, NJ: Educational Testing Service.

Topol, B., Olson, J., & Roeber, E. (2010). *The cost of new higher quality assessments: A comprehensive analysis of the potential costs for future state asssessments*. Stanford, CA: Stanford University, Stanford Center for Opportunity Policy in Education. Retrieved from edpolicy.stanford.edu/publications.pub/120

Topol, B., & Whitchurch, J. (2010). *Online assessment platform development recommendations: Building the next generation assessment platform—the consortia opportunity*. Retrieved from www.2.ed.gov/programs/racetothetop-assessment/rfi-response/asg-white-paper.pdf

U.S. Department of Education. (2008, April). *A nation accountable: Twenty-five years after a nation at risk.* Retrieved from http://www2.ed.gov/rschstat/research/pubs/accountable/accountable.pdf

U.S. Department of Education. (2010, March). *A blueprint for reform: The reauthorization of the elementary and secondary education act.* Washington, DC: Author.

Whitehurst, G. (2009). *Don't forget curriculum.* Washington, DC: Brookings Institution. Retrieved from www.brookings.edu/papers/2009/1014_curriculum_whitehurst.aspx

Whittier Union High School District. (2011). *Statement of beliefs.* Retrieved from http://www.wuhsd.org/site/Default.aspx?PageID=6

Williamson, R., & Blackburn, B. (2010). *Rigorous schools and classrooms: Leading the way.* Larchmont, NY: Eye On Education.

Willingham, D. (2009, September 28). *Reading is not a skill—and why this is a problem for the draft national standards.* Retrieved from The Answer Sheet at http://voices.washingtonpost.com/answer-sheet/daniel-willingham/willingham-reading-is-not-a-sk.html

# Index

# CORWIN
A SAGE Company

The Corwin logo—a raven striding across an open book—represents the union of courage and learning. Corwin is committed to improving education for all learners by publishing books and other professional development resources for those serving the field of PreK–12 education. By providing practical, hands-on materials, Corwin continues to carry out the promise of its motto: **"Helping Educators Do Their Work Better."**